PET BUGS

A KID'S GUIDE TO CATCHING AND KEEPING TOUCHABLE INSECTS

Sally Kneidel

Illustrated by Mauro Magellan

John Wiley & Sons, Inc.
New York • Chichester • Brisbane • Toronto • Singapore

I thank most of all my husband Ken who encouraged me,
edited every chapter, put all of it on the computer,
and added information here and there.
I appreciate the assistance of my children, Sarah and Alan,
in finding and feeding various insects, and helping me observe them.
I'm grateful also to the students and staff of Cotswold Elementary
in Charlotte, where I work, for the wonderful assortment of bugs
they bring me every day in peanut butter jars and shoe boxes.
Their eagerness is my fuel.

I thank Sally McMillan for her consistent support.

This text is printed on acid-free paper.

Copyright © 1994 by Sally Kneidel

Published by John Wiley & Sons, Inc.

Illustrations copyright © 1994 by Mauro Magellan

All rights reserved. Published simultaneously in Canada.

The publisher and the author have made every reasonable effort to insure
that the experiments and activities in this book are safe when conducted as
instructed but assume no responsibility for any damage caused or sustained
while performing the experiments or activities in this book. Parents,
guardians, and/or teachers should supervise young readers who undertake
the experiments and activities in this book.

Library of Congress Cataloging-in-Publication Data

Kneidel, Sally Stenhouse.
     Pet bugs: a kid's guide to catching and keeping touchable insects /
Sally Kneidel
          p. cm.
     ISBN 0-471-31188-X (paper : acid-free paper)
     1. Insects as pets—Juvenile literature. [1. Insects as pets. 2. Pets.] I.
Title.
SF459.I5K58   1994
638—dc20   93-39403

Printed in the United States of America

10 9 8 7

CONTENTS

*Walkingsticks are not predators, but are included in this section because of their relation to mantises.

INTRODUCTION_____

Why do young Monarch butterflies fly from Canada to Mexico every autumn, when other butterflies don't? Why do worker termites give up having their own children in order to serve their queen? Why do crickets chirp at one another and wrestle? Why do spittlebugs cover themselves with froth? Why are some Tiger Swallowtails brown, while most are yellow? There's always a reason, and figuring out the reason is the best part of science.

What's special about insects? For a person who likes to study nature, insects are very handy. They're everywhere! Count how many insects you see in one day. Pick a day when it's warm outdoors. You can probably spot 10 or 20 in a half hour, even if you live in the city. No other group of animals is so abundant. Three-fourths of all the animal species on earth are insects!

To some people, insects are bad news. Insects are often thought of, especially by adults, as things to squash or spray with poisons. The squashers and sprayers imagine insects crawling down blouses, diving into food, devouring gardens, or scuttling across pillows at night. And a few do. But most insects are much too busy with their own complex lives to bother with ours.

What sorts of complex lives? The aphid gives us one example. In summer, mother aphids produce only girl babies, who are born alive with their own tiny babies already inside them! Only girls are born all summer long until autumn, then males are born, too. Why should the aphid's reproduction be so odd? There's a very good reason, which you'll find in this book.

You'll also read a lot about insect behavior in this book. A neighbor of mine said she believed that fireflies blink because they're happy. Maybe in a Walt Disney movie, but not in nature! Nature is a dangerous place for animals, and they don't waste time and energy on unnecessary activities. Every animal behavior has developed because somehow it helps that animal or its children survive. Nearly everything animals do can be traced back to finding food, reproducing, and avoiding being eaten. Even "play" in young mammals usually involves practicing skills they'll need to survive.

How This Book Is Organized

Each chapter in this book covers a particular insect (or insect relative). The first section of each chapter tells you what the bug looks like. The second section describes where to find it. In the third and fourth sections, you'll find information about catching the bug and keeping it in captivity. The last section of each chapter tells you some interesting aspects of the bug's behavior.

In the Appendix you'll find a description of how insects are categorized by scientists—the classes, orders, and families of insects and some of their kin. The Appendix also describes insect anatomy, so you may refer to it often as you study the bugs described in each chapter. All of the terms used in this book that are in boldface type the first time they are used are listed in the Glossary.

A Few Pointers about Catching and Keeping Insects

1. **When you flip over logs or stones looking for bugs underneath, always return the log or stone to its original position.** It's home to many creatures you may not see. The dampness and crevices underneath are just as they like it. If you don't leave the log or stone as you found it, no creatures will be there the next time you look.

2. **If you put a creature in a jar to take indoors for a day or two, always place a slightly crumpled, damp (not wet) paper towel in the jar with it.** The paper towel will provide cracks and crevices for your creature to hide in and cling to. It will also provide moisture. Most of the dead insects that children bring to me in jars have died from lack of moisture. Your paper towel will need to be moistened daily with a few drops of water or a spray bottle.

   For many insects you can use plastic peanut butter jars (quart size) because they don't break if you drop them.

3. **To make a suitable lid for a jar, use a piece of cloth as a lid, held in place with a rubber band.** Plenty of air passes through cloth. If you don't believe it, hold your shirt over your mouth and breathe through it. And there are no small holes for tiny insects to escape through.

   If your pet bug clings to the cloth lid, thump the cloth before removing it. If a cloth lid is not readily available, you can ask your parents to poke holes in metal or plastic jar lids.

4. **Handle your pet bugs carefully.** Like all animals, insects respond well to gentle handling. A pinching grasp, between two fingers, is likely to injure most insects. And some insects, like the praying mantis, won't tolerate being grasped from behind. Generally you should let big insects, such as praying mantises and walkingsticks, stand on the back of your hand or arm. You don't want your fingertips moving around in a mantis's face. You might be mistaken for dinner. If a mantis or a walkingstick is on a stem, you may be able to get it to step onto the back of your hand by putting your hand in front of it.

5. **If you don't know what to feed your pet, don't keep it for more than a day or two.** If you don't see the insect eating after a day or two, let it go. Many people think that an insect is eating because it crawled

over the food or touched it. But if it is eating, you will see it holding the food or biting and chewing it. Insects eat with their mouths, just as you do. Don't let insects starve in their cages. Let them go if they don't eat.

If an insect is eating well, you can keep it for as long as you have the time to take care of it. Many insects have very short lives and will die soon no matter what you do. The life expectancy of most insects in nature is very short. Very few survive long enough to die of "old age." They're eaten by birds, toads, raccoons, other insects, and lots of other predators. They freeze and starve and get insect diseases, too. Your pet bug may very well live longer under your care than it would outside. But if you grow tired of it or can't remember to take care of it, let it go where you found it or in a similar place.

Insects You Should Not Pick Up

All the bugs listed in this book are safe to hold, but before you do, make sure it is the right bug. And make sure you hold it as directed. Lots of spiders bite, so leave them alone unless a parent helps you confirm that it's a jumping spider. Never pick up any shiny black spider; it could be a Black Widow.

Many species of ants bite or sting, even tiny ones. Velvet-ants are almost 1 inch (25 mm) long and look like they're covered with red velvet. The female is not winged and looks very much like an ant, although velvet-ants are really wasps. Females give a painful sting. They wander alone over the ground, not in groups like real ants. Of course, you know not to touch the ants' relatives, the bees and wasps.

There are several aquatic bugs and beetles that are predators and will bite or sting, such as giant water bugs and backswimmers. Avoid these and any beetlelike insect you find in water, unless you know it to be a safe one. Dragonfly larvae, which live in ponds, can pinch with their jaws.

Many of the predatory insects in the order Hemiptera (the true bugs) can give a painful bite. All hemipterans have a long, strawlike mouthpart. Those that are predators use the mouthpart to inject poison into their prey and suck up the body fluids. Hemipterans can be recognized by their "half-and-half" wings, which are thick at the base like those of a beetle, but thin and clear at the ends like those of a cicada or lacewing. Many hemipterans are plant suckers and don't bite. Some, such as giant water bugs and backswimmers, are aquatic. (The cicada and other homopterans—note the difference in spelling—have a similar mouthpart, but they are all plant suckers, have no poison, and don't bite.)

The assassin bug is one hemipteran in particular that you don't want to pick up. It's a slow-moving, sluggish bug, up to 1 inch (25 mm) long. Assassin bugs have an oddly long, thin head that projects out in front of the body and a downward curving beak. The sides of the abdomen stick out beyond the sides of the wings at rest, which is unusual in insects. Assassin bugs will stab and suck the juices from prey in a jar, such as darkling beetles. When the assassin bug is finished, its prey looks normal but is full of air inside. It feels like a piece of puffed rice.

Some beetles will bite. Before picking one up, touch it with a piece of cloth or blade of grass to see if it tries to bite. Look for pinching jaws.

Grasshoppers can give a sharp pinch with their jaws.

A few caterpillars have bristles that sting, particularly the Saddleback Caterpillar, which is green with a brown spot on the back.

This list doesn't cover everything that could bite or sting, only some of the more common ones. There are a number of useful field guides listed at the back of this book that can help you identify other bugs that might be dangerous to touch. But if in doubt, don't touch, just watch.

BUGS THAT EAT OTHER BUGS

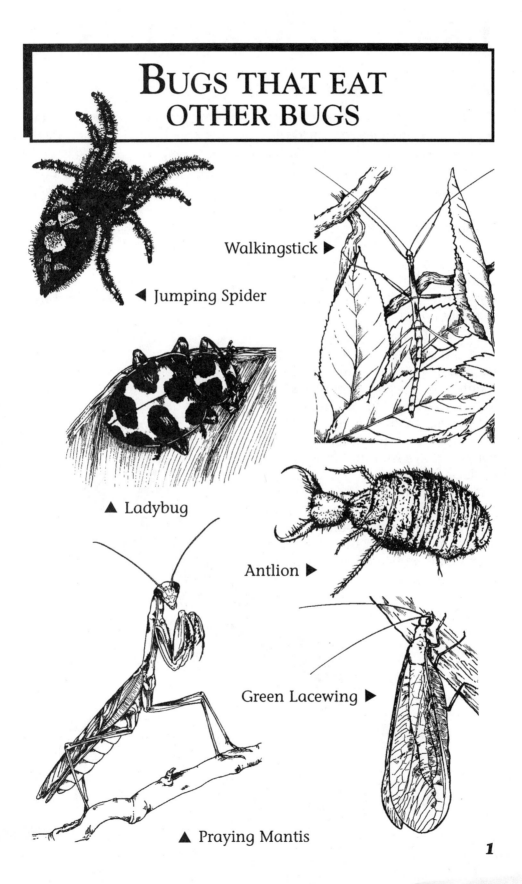

Walkingstick ▶

◀ Jumping Spider

▲ Ladybug

Antlion ▶

Green Lacewing ▶

▲ Praying Mantis

PRAYING MANTISES

What They Look Like

To recognize a mantis, look first for the two front legs held in front as if in prayer. These front legs are lined with spines to keep their victims, or **prey**, from slipping away. The back four legs are long, very thin walking legs.

Mantis bodies are long and green or brown. Their straight wings look like leaves and their long legs look like twigs, so they blend in very well with plants. A full-grown mantis is 3 to 4 inches (8 to 10 cm) long.

Praying mantises remind me a lot of the space creatures in the movie *Alien*. I think the aliens were modeled after mantises. And why not? For their size, mantises are perhaps the fiercest **predators**. A predator is an animal that kills and eats other animals. Wolves eat rabbits and mice, and so they're predators. Mantises are predators because they eat crickets and moths and other live insects.

A mantis has a triangular face with two big eyes and a little pointed mouth. The first time I saw a mantis up close I was surprised to see it turn its head to look at me. I've never seen another insect swivel its head like that. When a mantis looks you in the eye with that little pointed face and reaches out to climb onto your hand, the mantis seems like a smart and friendly little buddy. But the next moment it may attack and eat its brother! Such friendliness and fierceness together in one animal make the mantis a very interesting creature to get to know.

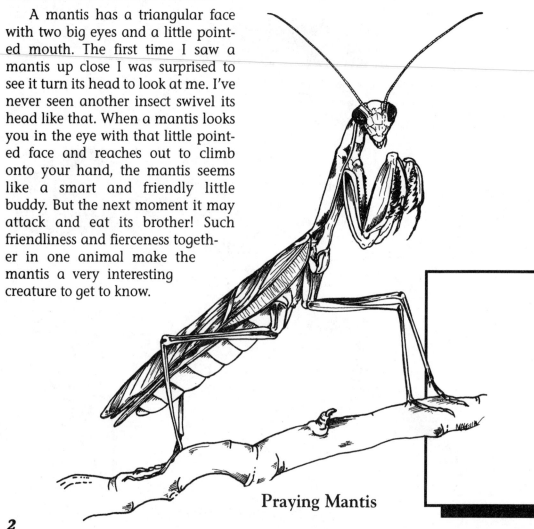

Praying Mantis

Where to Find Them

Mantises like to climb, so in summer I often find them up high on an outside wall or a porch. Mantises are hard to spot in nature because they're so well **camouflaged**—disguised or invisible by looking like the natural surroundings. But mantises' size makes them easy to see on human-made objects like window sills, cars, or lawn furniture. When I want to find a mantis, I just keep my eyes open and wait until one happens to be where I can see it.

If you can't find a mantis in your own backyard or park, you can order mantis egg cases from some biological supply catalogs (see Appendix). And once in a while I come across a mantis egg case stuck to a stem of tall grass, between knee- and waist height. It looks something like a light brown walnut, but weighs much less.

How to Catch Them

Since mantises like to climb, they will step onto a hand held just above and in front of them. They'll also step into a jar just slightly above them. Approaching a mantis can be hair-raising, but they are usually very easy to catch. I've held probably a hundred different mantises, usually on the back of my hand, and I've never known one to bite or try to bite. Just be sure to approach them slowly and handle them gently. If you're not sure about holding one, try wearing gloves.

Female mantises are easier to catch than males. In late summer females' tummies are swollen and round from the eggs inside, and they can't fly very well. But the male is pencil-thin and he may fly away as you approach, or as you handle him. I only keep females.

Class:	*Insecta*
Order:	*Orthoptera (orthopterans)*
Family:	*Mantidae (mantises only)*
Characteristics:	*Long, slim, green or brown body and long, thin legs. Triangular head that swivels. Front legs lined with spines and held as if in prayer.*
Distribution:	*Throughout the United States, into Ontario.*
Food:	*Live insects, especially crickets, flies, and moths.*

How to Keep Them

A mantis needs a **terrarium**, an enclosure for keeping and observing animals or plants indoors. A terrarium is usually made of clear plastic. It can be as small as 8 × 5 inches (20 × 13 cm) but larger is better—up to 10 × 20 inches (25 × 51 cm) or so. A lid is essential. A fiberglass windowscreen mesh lid is ideal because you can see through it and air flows through readily. You can buy these lids at pet stores. Or you can make a lid by just laying a rectangle of cloth over the top of the terrarium and taping the edges to the glass sides. A mantis won't try to squeeze under it. Don't use plastic wrap or glass lids, or the air inside will get foul with uneaten insect parts.

Keep the floor of the terrarium bare—no sand, no soil, no leaves—so the mantis's prey has nowhere to hide. Some predators will turn things over looking for prey, but mantises won't. The food has to be out in the open. All you need to put in the cage is a sturdy branched twig that won't rock. The mantis needs the twig to climb on.

Water the mantis by offering water in a spoon every day. It's fun to watch a mantis drink from a spoon. You'll feel like you've tamed a wild beast. Touch the water to her mouth if she doesn't notice it at first. Or you can water a mantis by spraying droplets in the cage daily with a mister.

If your mantis is a female, she may lay eggs on the twig in late summer or autumn. The eggs come out of the end of her body inside a mass of foam. The foam dries and hardens into a case. If you want to keep track of the hatchlings, put the twig with the egg case on it into a jar. Use a cloth lid secured with a rubber band. The egg case should not touch the sides of the jar. Keep the jar in the refrigerator, or else the eggs may hatch in midwinter when it's too cold to let them go outside. If you don't want to keep the egg case, put it in a bush outdoors. People who put the eggs in a jar outdoors usually forget about it and find a jar full of dead hatchlings months later.

If you keep the egg case in a jar in the refrigerator, take it out in March or April when insects begin to appear outdoors. One to four weeks later 10 to 100 baby mantises, or **nymphs,** will come out of the egg case. They look just like the adults but are only a little over ¼ inch (7 mm) long and have no wings. I recommend letting them go because they'll eat one another. If you want to keep one or two, offer it fruit flies and droplets from a mister. The baby mantis needs a small container at first or it won't be able to find the flies.

All adult mantises die in autumn or early winter no matter how well you care for them. Like the spider in *Charlotte's Web*, they leave their eggs to carry on.

What They Act Like

You can easily tell when a mantis is upset. She'll pull her front legs back against her body and draw her body back as a snake does before it strikes. If she's really upset, she'll flare her wings out to make herself look bigger and more menacing, just as a dog makes itself look bigger before a fight by making its hair stand up.

During my five years of handling mantises, I've never had one strike at me but I have seen them strike at moving objects that frighten them. I'm careful never to handle a mantis in such a way that it would want to strike at me. I always approach it slowly and let it step onto my hand at its own pace. I never approach or touch one from behind where it can't see me. And when a mantis is upset, I leave her alone until she calms down.

I did one time see a mantis grab someone's finger by accident, while striking at the prey the person was holding. The spines along the mantis's front legs sank into my friend's finger and drew blood. He yelled and tried to shake the mantis off, but she wouldn't let go. I had to grab the mantis and pull until she finally did let go. But don't let this scare you. Wear gloves if you feel nervous. I've fed them by hand dozens of times. You just have to be careful to hold the prey by the end of the back legs so that the prey's body is not right next to your finger. Your friends will be impressed, I guarantee it.

It is fun (and a little yucky) to watch a mantis eat a cricket. Silently and smoothly the mantis glides forward like a cat. Or an alien. Just before she strikes, the mantis rocks gently. Then bam. The strike takes only $\frac{1}{25}$ second. From the prayerful pose, the mantis unleashes its front legs in a lightning flash. The prey is grabbed, squeezed, and pierced by the spines that run up and down the mantis's front legs. There is no possibility of escape. Then (and here's the yucky part) the mantis eats the prey alive, tiny bite by tiny bite.

After munching for five to ten minutes, the mantis ends her meal and very delicately cleans herself. She pulls cricket parts off the spines and gently nibbles her front legs clean with her mouth. She cleans her face and eyes by nibbling at her front leg, then wiping the leg over her face just as a cat does. Finally, she cleans the delicate "feet" of her walking legs by holding them to her mouth. Her gentle, friendly self has returned...until it's mealtime again.

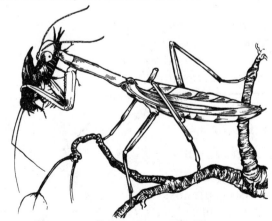

Praying Mantis with Prey

WALKINGSTICKS* _____

*Walkingsticks are not predators but are included here because of their relation to mantises.

What They Look Like

Imagine a twig that can walk! When the wind blows the branch, this animal "twig" sways along with all the real twigs. It's not only long and thin and twig-shaped, but it has the knobs, bumps, and color of a real twig as well. It may even have "leaves," that is, wings that look like leaves. This fantastic copy of a twig is called a walkingstick or stick insect. I thought mantises were great imitators of plant parts until I saw my first walkingstick. The walkingsticks win hands down.

The legs of walkingsticks are long and very spindly (like very thin twigs) and look as if they would break off easily. These creatures are *not* very good at walking, in spite of their name. They wobble like newborn colts. But they don't need to be good walkers. Since they eat tree leaves, their food is usually right in front of them.

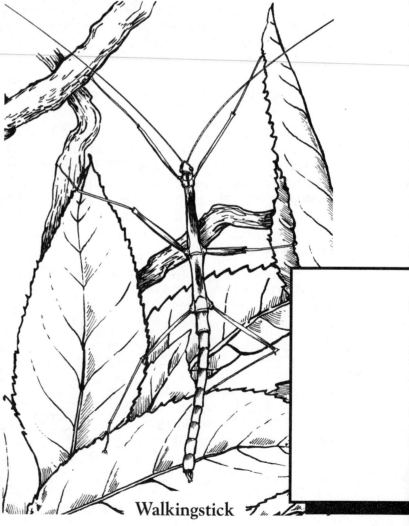

Most walkingsticks in the United States and Canada grow to about 2 or 3 inches (5 to 8 cm) long. One species in the southern United States, where they are more common, can grow up to 6 inches (15 cm) long. Green or brown is the usual color.

Walkingsticks are usually solitary creatures, but some species occur in crowds on trees. In large numbers they can be pests, eating all the leaves until the tree is bare.

Where to Find Them

Although some types of insects are just as common in cities as

Walkingstick

in the country, walkingsticks are not. I have found walkingsticks most often in structures near deep forests—for example, in a bathroom at a campground. Like the mantises, the walkingsticks I have found have always been on surfaces that weren't plants, such as sidewalks or buildings. That's because their camouflage doesn't work on human-made backgrounds. I can't set out to find a walkingstick and expect to come across one. I have to wait until I stumble upon one by accident.

How to Catch Them

Walkingsticks are easy to pick up. But handle them carefully, because their little stick legs are so fragile. Some walkingsticks will go rigid and drop from their perches if you disturb them, but if you move very slowly and place your hand in front of the walkingstick, it will eventually step onto your hand as if it were another branch.

There are hundreds of species of walkingsticks, and most live in the tropics (the very hot regions of the world). Some of these species have odd ways of defending themselves. They are creatures you wouldn't want to pick up. They could throw up on you, spray chemicals at you,

Catching a Walkingstick

Class:	*Insecta*
Order:	*Orthoptera (orthopterans)*
Family:	*Phasmatidae (walkingsticks only)*
Characteristics:	*Twiglike bodies with six long, thin legs.*
Distribution:	*Throughout the United States, north to Alberta. More common in the South.*
Food:	*Leaves of black cherry, oak, hickory, walnut, or locust trees or other trees on which it is found.*

or jab you with their leg spines. Or they might flash brightly colored wings to startle you. But the common walkingsticks of the United States and Canada are wingless and spineless, and have no defenses. None bite or sting.

How to Keep Them

Walkingsticks can live for several months in a terrarium. All they need to eat is the leaves of trees and shrubs. Most are very picky about what type of leaves they'll eat and how the leaves are offered. I have fed mine a combination of oak leaves, hickory leaves, and black cherry leaves. You might try locust or walnut leaves, too. The tree you find them on is probably a type they like to eat.

You can't just lay a few leaves on the terrarium floor. Walkingsticks are used to climbing on twigs as they eat. Put a couple of freshly cut twigs with several leaves on each into a small glass of water in the terrarium. These branches take up room, so a 10 × 20 inch (25 × 51 cm) glass aquarium is a good size, but smaller will do. Of course, you need a lid for the terrarium or the walkingstick will climb out. A cloth or windowscreen mesh lid is good for air circulation. See the section on "Keeping Mantises" in the previous chapter for a description of how to make such a lid. Pet stores sell plastic terraria with plastic lids that provide good ventilation.

Walkingsticks are used to drinking water in the form of dew or rain droplets, so water your pet by spraying the leaves daily or offering a drop on your fingertip. They may drink from a dish. The twigs must be changed every day or so. Your stick buddy won't eat old ones.

You can see them munching the edges of the leaves in much the same way caterpillars do. It's easy to tell which leaves have already been munched. Walkingsticks tend to eat a little of one leaf and move on, without finishing the first one.

Walkingsticks won't eat each other as mantises will, so you can keep several together. Walkingsticks kept indoors will die in the autumn, which is common in adult insects. They've done their duty by making eggs to overwinter, and food will soon be in short supply or nonexistent.

What They Act Like

The mantis and the walkingstick may be cousins, but in some ways they're as different as Frankenstein and a fairy princess. Their differences stem from the fact that the mantis is a predator, or killer of other animals, while the walkingstick is a peaceful and harmless vegetarian. One is designed to kill, and one is designed strictly for hiding—to avoid *being* killed.

First, let's look at their similarities, and they do have some. After all, they're both in the insect order Orthoptera, along with crickets and grasshoppers. Both walkingsticks and mantises are long and thin, green or brown, and look like plant parts. Both are well camouflaged on trees or shrubs. Both have **cerci**, or feelers, on the back end of the abdomen. Both tend to freeze when disturbed, throwing their front legs forward and together to look more twiglike.

But the predatory and the vegetarian way of life have led to some very different body parts and behaviors. The mantis's two front legs are very different from its four twiggy back legs. The front two have developed, sharp spines and very strong muscles for grabbing and holding prey.

The walkingstick has no need for strong grasping legs, and so all six of its legs are very much like the back legs of the mantis—very skinny walking legs. And though they look like the strong back legs of the mantis, they're actually much weaker.

Because the mantis needs to be able to track and follow its prey—a fly or a beetle—it has evolved the unusual ability to turn its head freely. Very few insects can turn their heads. The mantis has also developed large **compound eyes** made up of many separate visual units for watching prey. It has to be able to judge the distance to its prey to make a good strike.

The walkingstick doesn't need to see much of anything except the next leaf or twig. It has no need for turning its small head, and can't. The eyes on the walkingstick are much smaller than those of a mantis, because its food is always right in front of it and doesn't need to be captured. The walkingstick is designed for a still and passive life, while the mantis is made for action.

The way walkingsticks and mantises make their babies is a little different, too, although this is probably not related to their different ways of feeding. A female mantis makes one big egg mass out of foam, which is fixed to a twig. A female walkingstick lays her eggs one at a time. Each egg looks very much like a plant seed. She flings them with the end of her body or just drops them. The eggs fall on the forest floor under the tree in which the mama lives and eats. So when they hatch all they have to do is climb and they'll be on the right kind of tree.

Both walkingstick and mantis eggs hatch into nymphs. The nymphs of both mantises and walkingsticks have a natural urge to walk upward toward light, which takes them into the leaves of the tree. This urge is an inherited and automatic behavior, or **instinct**. An instinctive behavior develops in a very predictable way within a particular species.

The walkingstick and mantis show us how nature can take similar body plans and change them in different directions to suit different insects' ways of life.

JUMPING SPIDERS

What They Look Like

Jumping spiders are different animals from your usual spiders. For one thing, they have short stocky legs, instead of the long spindly legs of most spiders. Jumpers are usually less than ½ inch (12 mm) long. Some are as brightly colored as parrots, with long tufts of hair here and there that can look like eyebrows or bushy hairdos.

A sure way to tell jumping spiders from other types of spiders is by the eyes. Each jumper has two very big eyes on the front of its head, two smaller eyes beside the big ones, and four very small ones farther back. So it can see almost all the way around its body! No other spider has the two large eyes that occupy most of its "face."

Another thing that sets jumping spiders apart is their behavior. Unlike most spiders, they don't build webs to catch prey , but rather strut around on those short, thick legs like heavyset boxers, flexing their muscles and looking for a tumble. Look, too, for the irregular pace of the walk—quick starts, stops, and jumps.

The jumping spider is in some ways like a small tiger. It's as furry and cuddly as a little tiger, and it wanders through the woods, searching for prey—another animal to attack and eat for supper. Its big eyes scan the ground and the air, searching for movement. Something is flying by! Our friend flings itself into the air—and makes the catch—just like a tiger. But this little guy has six eyes and four legs too many to be a tiger!

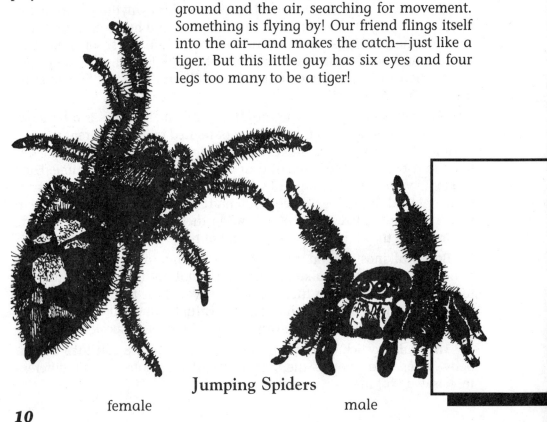

Jumping Spiders

female   male

Where to Find Them

You usually see jumping spiders on high places. They like to climb because a high perch helps them leap on flying insects. You'll find them on tabletops (indoors and out), on the tops of fence posts, on clothesline poles, and on faucets sticking up out of the ground. There's a metal fence around the ballfield behind my house and two out of three fence posts have jumping spiders on top.

They don't hide in dark, dusty places the way Black Widows and some other scary spiders do. Jumpers like the sun—they hunt and wander about in daylight. No lurking behind books or papers either. Wide open spaces are okay for this brave little spider. Since they're not web builders, you won't find them in webs. They do sometimes build silken nests though. More about that in a moment.

How to Catch Them

You can catch a jumping spider by letting it step onto your fingers, or by putting a jar over it and sliding a piece of paper under the jar. Although jumping spiders have fangs like all spiders do, they don't bite humans. Since some spiders do bite, always check with an adult to make sure it is a jumper before you pick up any spider. Never pick up an all black, shiny spider; it may be a Black Widow.

How to Keep Them

Jumpers do well in captivity. Since they can climb anything, you must have a secure lid on your container. I've kept them in small terraria—4 × 7 inches (10 × 18 cm)—and in large jars with cloth lids. On a jar you

Class:	*Arachnida (spiders, mites, and their kin)*
Order:	*Araneae (spiders)*
Family:	*Salticidae (jumping spiders only)*
Characteristics:	*Active during the day; stocky; walk at an irregular pace; jump. Two large eyes on the front of the face.*
Distribution:	*Throughout the United States and Canada.*
Food:	*Live insects.*

can secure the lid with a rubber band. On a small terrarium a cloth lid can be pulled tightly over the edges and taped to the sides. The lid must be tighter than for mantises or walkingsticks because the jumping spider will squeeze through gaps, where the other two won't.

The difficult part of keeping them is that they must have live prey regularly, every other day or so. Fruit flies will do as dinner, since most jumpers are small spiders. (A later chapter describes how to catch fruit flies.) Try any little creature that's smaller than your pet. Like all spiders, jumpers poison their prey with their fangs and then suck out the insides, leaving an empty skin behind. A fairly big meal may keep your spider full for several days. I've never seen a spider drink, but you can offer water droplets.

Your jumping spider may build a small silken house with two doors in its container. This is not a cocoon but a nest that the spider moves in and out of freely. The nest may be a hiding place where the spider can shed its outgrown skin, or it may mean your spider needs a hiding place for her egg sac. She'll guard the babies until they're ready to move out on their own. Hatchlings are *tiny* and can get through small spaces. They may manage to escape from the container.

What They Act Like

Jumping spiders can see motion to the side and behind with the very small eyes on each side of their head. They can see much better than any other spider. Because jumpers hunt their prey by stalking (following them), they need good eyesight. Their big eyes can see objects that are still, not just those in motion. Other hunting spiders, like the wolf spider, can see only moving prey. Spiders that make webs *feel* their prey through the silk lines and can barely see at all. Scientists have figured this out by testing what sorts of things different spiders react to.

Jumping Spider Jumping onto a Stick

You can prove to yourself that jumpers can see well. Put your jumper on a tabletop and slowly move a finger on the table behind the spider. Once you have the jumper's attention, it'll freeze and—this is what's fun to watch—it'll bend its body around so that the big eyes in front are fixed squarely on your finger, like the headlights of a car. Although a jumper has good eyesight, it can't move its eyes nearly as well as you can. That's why it must turn its whole body to see you.

Jumping spiders use their eyesight not only to catch prey but also to fight other males. Mature jumping spiders also use ther eyesight in **courtship**, any behavior that signals mating readiness. If you catch two jumpers of the same species, you may get to see the male flinging up his hairy arms and turning his body at funny angles to get a female's attention. Some males will do this even to the image of a female on a computer screen! Will a female find him as daring and interesting as we do? Will she marvel at his great big black eyes?

No, it takes a person, maybe a budding biologist like yourself, to fully appreciate the talents of the jumper. This is a different sort of spider, one who wanders freely in the sun in search of prey. It has no need of a web— its good eyes and strong legs are tools enough for the job.

ANTLIONS

What They Look Like

The largest of antlions could rest on your thumbnail. They range in length from ⅛ inch (3 mm) to almost ½ inch (13 mm). The frightful head is flat and squarish; the body, light brown and oval, rounded across the back. Being insects, they have six legs, but four stay tucked under the body where you can't see them from above.

When you meet an antlion for the first time, you might imagine you're meeting a knight of long ago—a deadly fighter whose jaws look like two needle-sharp swords. Would you like to watch him charge his victim? He's fearless, although his opponent may be twice his size. Look at him go! With his two fierce weapons, he pierces his foe.

But wait a minute, where's his armor? Hey, this guy's still in his underwear! And say, isn't he a little plump to be a knight? Well, yes, our little knight *is* a bit soft. And in truth a little slow. His swordlike jaws may be awesome, but his pale, pudgy body wouldn't scare a flea.

That's okay, he has exactly what he needs to be an antlion, if not a real knight. This guy uses his jaws to catch *dinner,* not to win battles. When he's waiting to ambush a dinner victim, his plump, vulnerable little body lies quietly hidden under the sand. Only his fearsome weapons, his jaws, are out in the open. Once he's nailed some unfortunate bug, the antlion injects poison into the luckless creature, then sucks out the bug's insides. *Yuck!* But what may be liquid guts to us is the antlions's bread and butter.

Where to Find Them

Antlions live in pits in sand or loose soil, so the pit is what to look for. The antlion itself lies under the sand at the bottom of the pit, with only its jaws sticking out. Try sandy areas, such as a sand dune at the beach or a sandy playground. You might find one under part of a play structure that's close to, but not touching the ground. They may be under a

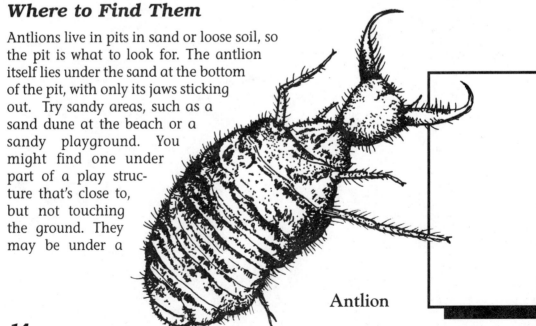

Antlion

seldom-used park bench or picnic table. Sometimes pits are made in areas of loose dry soil instead of sand. Antlion pits are usually in places human feet never go.

The pit is a perfect cone shape, as though someone had taken a cone-shaped drinking cup and pushed the point of it down into the sand until the top of the cup was level with the ground. The antlion's pit, though, is much smaller than a cup, ½ to 3 inches (1 to 8 cm) across at the top, and up to 1½ inches (4 cm) deep. I sometimes mistake drip marks in the sand for antlion pits, but a pit is pointed at the bottom, while drip marks are rounded at the bottom.

Jaws of Antlion at Base of Pit

How to Catch Them

Catching antlions is easy, since they make no effort to get away. Once you've found a pit, get a spoon and scoop deep under the bottom point of the pit. Do this carefully since the antlion sits just under the lowest part of the pit and you don't want to injure your foundling. Put the scooped-out pit into a bowl or on a newspaper and jiggle it gently. You'll see the little creature in the shallow sand. Instead of trying to pick it up with your fingers, slide paper under it or pour it into your hand. Although the jaws look dangerous, antlions won't bite. They use the jaws only to capture prey, not for defense. They defend themselves by staying hidden.

Class:	*Insecta*
Order:	*Neuroptera (neuropterans)*
Family:	*Myrmeleontidae (antlions only)*
Characteristics:	*Larvae live at the base of a cone-shaped pit in sand or loose, dry soil. Adults are brown, long, and slim, with clear, veined wings and long, knobbed antennae.*
Distribution:	*Throughout the United States. Most common in the South and Southwest.*
Food:	*Larvae eat ants or other small, nonflying insects that fall into their pits.*

How to Keep Them

You can keep an antlion indoors or out. To keep one indoors, fill a deep soup bowl with fine sand—no lumps or pebbles or plant pieces mixed in. Smooth the surface so it's flat, and put the antlion on top. If the sand is small-grained and loose, the antlion will dig a new pit within a day or two. Don't try to dig the pit yourself or help the antlion dig it; you can't. The bowl doesn't need a lid because the antlion won't leave the sand. You can keep several together, but you'll need a bigger container than a bowl. At my house we have a box for antlions that is about 4 inches deep (10 cm) and 15 inches (38 cm) square. The sand in it is about 2 to 3 inches (5 to 8 cm) deep. About ten antlions have made pits in the box.

Feed your antlion an ant or fruit fly or some other very small bug every day. If you think you might forget, make a spot outdoors for it so it can find its own meal. Dig a hole 3 inches (8 cm) deep in an out-of-the-way place. Fill the hole with fine sand and put the antlion on top. If you put an occasional apple core near the pit, plenty of ants will probably come to fill your guest's larder.

The antlion that lives in the sand is actually a larva. The larval stage can last as long as three years! When it reaches almost ½ inch (1 cm) in length, it makes a silken ball around itself, called a cocoon. Inside the silken structure, the antlion goes through complete **metamorphosis**, or an abrupt, great change in shape, like a caterpillar turning into a butterfly. This stage of life in the cocoon is the pupal stage, and the antlion is called a pupa.

If your antlion disappears from its pit in the spring, sift through the sand and you may find the little silken ball, about ⅜ to ½ inch (9 to 12 mm) in diameter, coated with sand. Leave it in the sand outdoors, so that when the adult comes out it can find a mate and lay eggs. The adult is about 1 to 1¼ inch (25 to 30 mm) long and brown. The clear wings and long slender body are somewhat like that of the lacewing, although not as pretty, delicate-looking, or as wide. The two are closely related, both being in the order Neuroptera.

What They Act Like

An antlion has a strong instinct to dig. If you put one in the palm of your hand with a little sand, it will begin right away to wiggle its rear end into the sand and walk backward. The antlion is trying to cover its soft plump body with sand so you won't eat it. The wiggling makes nice tickles in the palm of your hand. In deeper sand, your little friend may hide at first but will soon begin the serious business of making a pit. This is a wonderful thing to watch.

The antlion walks backward in a circle, waggling its rear end to get its body under the sand, then flicking the sand to one side with its head. It makes a spiral path inward and downward, making smaller and smaller circles as the sand flies out. If the antlion is in a bowl, you can hear some of the sand hit the rim and watch the rest of it sail out onto the table. By the time the little digger reaches the end of the spiral, it has made a pit and is under the center point of the cone. Only the jaws are visible, open wide and waiting. I've watched antlions make pits many times and it always puzzles me how they get the sides so smooth and even.

Now the fun begins. If an ant makes the mistake of wandering into a pit, it usually slides all the way down to the bottom of the pit, where it meets the open jaws of the antlion. The jaws clamp shut on the ant and that's that. But the antlion never leaves the bottom of the pit to come after the ant. So the ant is safe if it can somehow avoid sliding all the way to the bottom. And it tries, oh, it tries. Its frantic legs flail at the sand, trying to climb up the slippery sides.

The whole process is very similar to the way most spiders catch and eat dinner. A spider's web is a prey trap just as the antlion's pit is. And like spiders, the antlion poisons its prey and sucks out the insides. But while many people are spooked by spiders, few are afraid of this insect in spite of its sharp jaws. The antlion's plump body and short legs just don't look very creepy, and after all, to us the jaws are quite tiny. But from an ant's point of view those jaws are a different matter—needle-sharp swords that mean to rob the ant of its insides. A scary proposition, even if the owner of the jaws is a pudgy little guy who forgot his armor.

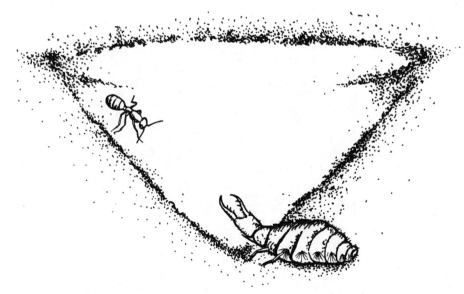

Ant Falling into Antlion Pit

LADYBUGS OR LADYBIRD BEETLES

What They Look Like

There are lots of different species of ladybugs, or ladybird beetles, and each has a different color pattern. The two hard wings, or **elytra**, that cover the back are red or yellow or orange with black spots, or else black with red to yellow spots. Some have two spots, some have many more. Some have no spots at all.

A ladybug looks like a pretty button or sequin. It's probably the most easily recognized of all 300,000 species of beetles. So pretty, it must be gentle and sweet; as the nursery rhyme says:

> *Ladybug, ladybug, fly away home,*
> *Your house is on fire and your children are alone.*

A devoted mama, tending those young ones—and crunching other animals to death with her strong jaws. (Of course, some ladybugs are male. I say "she" because of the name.)

Don't look for mama ladybug in her children's nursery. Jurassic Park instead! This little spangled jewel looks innocent enough. She has no spiny legs for grabbing like a mantis or long sharp jaws like an antlion. But she's deadly nonetheless. (How do they manage being predators without such equipment? More about that in a moment.)

Ladybug

Where to Find Them

Ladybugs hang out where the food is. Their favorite lunch is aphids (described in a later chapter), so that means they're on garden plants such as lettuce and tomato plants, and on weeds and shrubs. Occasionally, you can spot a ladybug on the ground or somewhere other than a plant. But if you're looking for them, look on plants.

How to Catch Them

Ladybugs are one of the few flying insects that will allow themselves to be picked up, so they're relatively easy to catch. You're less likely to injure a ladybug if you brush it onto your palm rather than pick it up by pinching it between thumb and fingertip. If you have one in hand, you have only a few seconds to get it into a container before it flies away.

How to Keep Them

Keep ladybugs in small containers so that they can find their dinner. A jar or a 4 × 7 inch (10 × 18 cm) plastic terrarium works well. A cloth lid secured with a rubber band allows good ventilation. If you put in a dish of water, she may drown, so it's better to water her with a wet piece of paper towel or wet cotton swab. She can suck out the moisture she needs. If you're going to carry the container around, don't put in rocks or sticks or soil, or your ladybug may be crushed.

To feed her, put in a small twig that has aphids on it, or you can use a small paintbrush to knock aphids off the twig into the container. The

Class:	*Insecta*
Order:	*Coleoptera (beetles)*
Family:	*Coccinellidae (ladybugs only)*
Characteristics:	*Almost round beetles, usually brightly colored. Yellow to red with black spots, or black with yellow to red spots. Head almost hidden. Larvae are very small, spiny, and caterpillarlike, but walk much faster than caterpillars.*
Distribution:	*Throughout North America.*
Food:	*Both adults and larvae eat aphids and scale insects, which are plant pests.*

ladybug needs to be fed every day. A single ladybug can go through a huge number of aphids—100 or more a day. But she will survive on only a few a day. You can keep several ladybugs in one container, but because they eat so much, one is probably enough. Keep her as long as you have the energy to keep her well fed.

After a female mates, she lays eggs on a plant where there are aphids. The eggs look like tiny yellow cigars, all standing on end in a cluster. They hatch into spiny little gray or black larvae that look like very fast, humpbacked caterpillars. They're tiny at first, but grow quickly to about ¼ inch (6 mm) in length. Because they're growing so fast, they eat even more aphids than their parents.

**Ladybugs Eating Aphids
on Rose**

What They Act Like

A ladybug can't eat a blade of grass or a crumb of cake. She can only eat living animals. And she can't eat just any animals, even if they are the right size. Ladybugs eat primarily aphids. They also eat **scale insects**, small homopterans that feed on plants as aphids do. Many scale insects are legless, stay in one spot, and have a scalelike covering, hence the name.

It's unusual for a predator to be as particular about what it eats as the ladybug is. Most predators will eat any animal they can catch. They can't afford to be picky because predators often don't get enough to eat. (Having a limited amount of food keeps predator populations from growing very big.)

But ladybugs *are* picky, very picky. I've offered them wingless fruit flies, which are about the same size as most aphids. Wingless fruit flies can't fly and should be fairly easy for ladybugs to catch. But ladybugs won't eat them, won't even try.

Very few predators are as picky as the ladybug. This pickiness is a form of **specialization**, which means restriction of an animal's activities to a portion of the environment. The ladybug's specialization is limiting its diet to only one or two types of prey. It might be risky for a predator like an owl to prey only on field mice because there's a good chance the owl wouldn't find enough field mice to keep it alive. But for ladybugs aphids are a pretty safe bet. A mother aphid makes huge numbers of babies in a short period of time, and all of her children quickly grow up and make more babies, so that the plant often becomes covered with aphids. When a ladybug finds an aphid, she usually finds hundreds.

Aphids are not only abundant, they also have little means of defense. They are soft-bodied and they can't fly or run. This suits ladybugs well because they have no way to fight or restrain their prey. Unlike a praying mantis, a ladybug doesn't have grasping legs. All six of her legs are designed for walking only. A ladybug can walk right up to an aphid and take a bite without ever touching the aphid in any other way.

Although a ladybug may sometimes place a "foot" on an aphid as if to hold it down, her small jaws are really her only means of attack. This may not work with other potential prey such as fruit flies, which walk faster and are not so soft. A ladybug eating an aphid is like a person eating a wad of cotton candy on a table. You could take a bite without using your hands. But if a self-propelled apple rolled by (this is what a fruit fly would seem like to a ladybug), taking a bite would be a lot harder.

The ladybug moves down a branch covered with aphids like a slow-moving lawn mower. The aphid's way of surviving these lawn mowers is to make more, more, and more aphids. As the predator munches, the prey cranks out replacements. In nature they stay in balance.

GREEN LACEWINGS_____

What They Look Like

With her long slender body and delicate gauzy wings, the lacewing seems a visitor from fairy land or heaven. Lacewing children, on the other hand, are such vicious little devils that they'll stab and eat each other if no other victims are in sight. The netlike or lacelike appearance of an adult lacewing's clear wings is due to the crisscrossing of tiny veins. At rest, the wings are folded along the body like a steep pitched roof, their edges forming a ridge down the insect's back. Compare this to the wings of a beetle, fly, or mantis, which lie flat along their backs. A lacewing larva has a soft, alligatorlike body (wider in the middle) and long thin jaws that look like curved needles.

Green lacewings are the most common type of lacewing. They are pale green all over, and ½ to ¾ inch (13 to 19 mm) in length as adults. A brown variety is less common. Lacewings are neuropterans, an order that also includes antlions. Adult antlions look similar to lacewings except that they're bigger and brown and not as pretty.

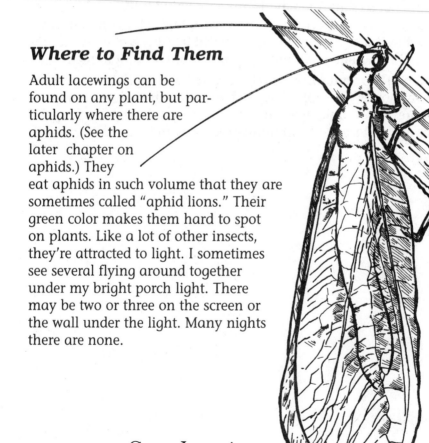

Where to Find Them

Adult lacewings can be found on any plant, but particularly where there are aphids. (See the later chapter on aphids.) They eat aphids in such volume that they are sometimes called "aphid lions." Their green color makes them hard to spot on plants. Like a lot of other insects, they're attracted to light. I sometimes see several flying around together under my bright porch light. There may be two or three on the screen or the wall under the light. Many nights there are none.

Green Lacewing

22

How to Catch Them

The easiest way to catch green lacewings is by leaving on a porch light on a summer evening. If you have a strong porch light, you may be able to see one well enough to catch it in midair with a jar. If you have one on your screen at night, simply put a jar over it and slide a piece of cardboard between jar and screen. You'll have to do this slowly to avoid sending the bug into flight.

Lacewings around Porch Light

How to Keep Them

A jar with a lid made of cloth and held in place with a rubber band may make a better home than a terrarium. If the lacewings have *too* much room they may not be able to find their dinner. Keep a damp piece of paper towel in the container for moisture.

In captivity, a lacewing will eat as many aphids or other tiny soft-bodied insects as you can feed it. It is easier to offer an aphid-covered twig than to count out aphids one by one. Some lacewing species may not feed at all, their lives being too brief to need nourishment.

Class:	*Insecta*
Order:	*Neuroptera (neuropterans)*
Family:	*Chrysopidae (green lacewings only)*
Characteristics:	*Wings clear and veined, greenish, forming a peak over the back. Eyes golden or copper-colored. Larvae are canoe-shaped and tiny, with long, thin, curving jaws.*
Distribution:	*Throughout North America.*
Food:	*Both larvae and adults eat aphids.*

What They Act Like

Mama lacewing lays her eggs individually, each on its own hair-thin, stiff little stalk. The eggs don't look like eggs, but rather like tiny egg-shaped golf balls on very long golf tees, or like balloons on long strings. The stalk and egg together are probably not more than ¼ inch (6 mm) tall. The lacewing makes this peculiar structure by dabbing her abdomen onto a leaf (or deck railing or tree), leaving a blob of self-made glue, and quickly pulling her abdomen up, as you might pull a piece of caramel or gum into a long string. The hardening glue stretches into a long stalk. The lacewing then leaves a tiny, pale green or gray egg on top. What is amazing is that both stalk and egg are so perfectly formed, and so very tiny and delicate.

Lacewings put the eggs on stalks to protect them from predators. Ladybugs and ladybug larvae, as well as other lacewings, live on the same plants and eat aphids. Since the eggs are about the same size as a small aphid, and are as still as aphids, they could very well be eaten. The stalk probably keeps the lacewing eggs just out of reach of these aphid munchers.

Lacewing hatchlings begin as larvae and are gray and very tiny at first, smaller than the head of a pin. They look like a cross between a caterpillar and an alligator! These blood-thirsty little beasts use their long hollow jaws to puncture the bodies of aphids and other soft-bodied insects. Through the jaws, a poison is injected into the prey that paralyzes it, and then the body juices are sucked out. The puncture-and-suck way of feeding is similar to that of antlions and spiders.

I once raised a lacewing larva. It was no larger than a flea when I found it on my back deck. I kept it on the kitchen table in a little, clear plastic dish with a clear plastic lid. (They are so tiny that lifting the lid once a day provided enough fresh air.) I fed it *tiny* tent caterpillars (discussed in a later chapter), and **maggots** (fly larvae) from a single mushroom brought in from the yard. When the lacewing larva grabbed a caterpillar, the victim wiggled and squirmed, but never got away. After two to three hours, the caterpillar was completely drained—a shriveled, shrunken shell. The little lacewing larva thrived, and after a week or two made a tiny silken cocoon on the side of the dish. The cocoon was a perfect ball, the size of a tomato seed. Inside, the little creature got busy turning into an adult. Ten days after it made the cocoon, a delicate fairylike lacewing with pale green wings emerged. I let it go on the deck, to find one of its own and mate before its short life was over.

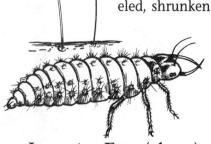

**Lacewing Eggs (above)
and Larva**

BUGS THAT HAVE SPECIAL TRICKS TO AVOID BEING GOBBLED UP

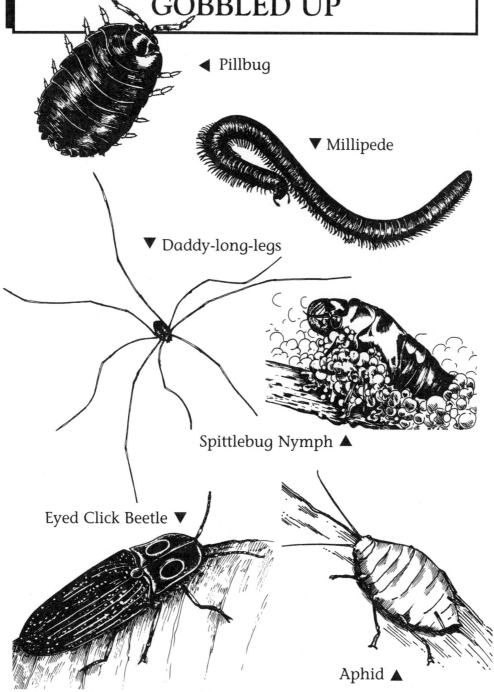

◀ Pillbug

▼ Millipede

▼ Daddy-long-legs

Spittlebug Nymph ▲

Eyed Click Beetle ▼

Aphid ▲

APHIDS

What They Look Like

Aphids come in lots of different colors. The most common ones in my garden are green or red. The narrower end is the head, with very tiny eyes and antennae. The six legs are so thin you can barely see them. If you watch aphids carefully you'll have a chance to watch an animal being born. The tiny babies come right out of the mother's body just as little humans do. There's no doctor to catch them, of course, and no need for one. The baby aphids hit the ground running; that is, ready to move around and eat.

Aphids are nature's baby factories. What they lack in size, they make up for in number. Armies of aphids! For most people, these armies are not welcome visitors. They make a living sucking the juices out of plants with their straw-like mouthparts that they poke into the tender new leaves. And lots of their plant victims are gardeners' favorites, like lettuce. A horde of aphids can suck dry a tall plant and kill it. Adults are often no bigger than the head of a pin. A newborn aphid can be as small as a period at the end of a sentence.

Aphids are the munchkins of the animal world. They're all over the lettuce in my garden and they're so tiny I can't get them all off. (I probably eat dozens of aphids every day in my salad without knowing it!) They're not only tiny, but very soft. Being soft makes aphids tasty dinners for other insects, such as ladybugs (see the earlier chapter on ladybugs).

Where to Find Them

Because aphids are so munchable, they often hide on the undersurface of leaves. They like new leaves best, and new stems and buds. Look at the tops of plants and tips of branches where the new leaves start. If there's a vegetable garden nearby, check there first—especially lettuce plants, tomato plants, and pea or bean plants. You won't find aphids on every plant, but when you do find them, you'll usually see a lot.

I seldom find aphids on trees, but sometimes you'll see them on shrubs or weeds. Thistle and goldenrod are favorites. If you see a ladybug on a plant, investigate. Aphids are probably what drew her there.

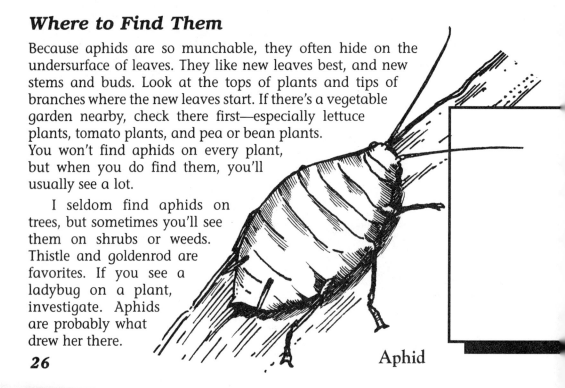

Aphid

How to Catch Them

You can lift aphids with a cotton swab or a small paintbrush without injuring them. When you scoop them up from the side, their legs get tangled for a moment in the fibers or bristles. Then tap the brush or cotton swab with your finger and the aphid will fall off into the palm of your other hand. Can you feel it walking? Just barely, if at all. Put it on the back of your arm and watch it struggle through the hair jungle. Does it tickle?

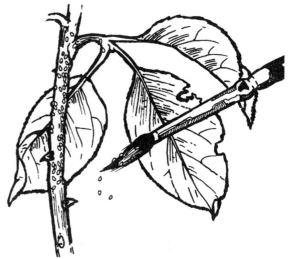

Catching Aphids with a Paintbrush

Aphids can be tricky to catch, though. Now you see them, now you don't. Their soft bodies make them very vulnerable to predators, so their best defense is getting away fast. They'll drop from a leaf and vanish at the slightest disturbance. If you touch the aphid once with a paintbrush and don't get it, you won't get another chance. It'll be gone! So approach the aphid from underneath, or hold your hand or container underneath so that if the aphid drops you'll catch it.

How to Keep Them

Aphids will survive without food for a day or so in a jar with a damp paper towel for moisture and a cloth lid secured with a rubber band. But if you want to keep them longer than that, you need to have a potted

Class:	*Insecta*
Order:	*Homoptera (homopterans)*
Family:	*Aphididae (aphids only)*
Characteristics:	*Pear-shaped, tiny, soft-bodied, almost always with a pair of sticklike projections off rear of body, called* **cornicles.** *Often green or red, but may be other colors. Some with wings, most without wings. Found on plants.*
Distribution:	*Throughout North America.*
Food:	*Plant sap.*

plant of the same type as the one the aphid came from. Aphids won't stay on plucked leaves. The sap in the plant must be flowing, so the plant must be rooted. Some aphids are picky and like only a few types of plants.

The plant doesn't need to be in a container, other than the pot it's rooted in. If it's healthy and the right kind of plant, the aphids will stay on it. If not, just put the plant outdoors. If the aphids become crowded, they may produce babies with wings, who will fly in search of new plants.

What They Act Like

The most interesting thing about aphids is how they make their families. You are like your father in some ways—maybe the color of your eyes or the shape of your feet—and like your mother in other ways. That's because most mothers have to find a male to mate with before they can have offspring (children). But aphid babies are exact copies of their mothers because they have no fathers. Aphid mothers don't need to mate.

In the spring and summer, aphid mothers make only girl babies, no boys. When these female babies are only one week old, they begin giving birth to their own babies, all female. In fact, babies when born already carry babies within them! So if you put a single aphid on a plant, pretty soon you'll have a lot more.

In the autumn the aphids' reproduction changes in preparation for winter. The aphids give birth to males and females, who mate with each other. These new females then lay eggs instead of giving birth to more young. The eggs can survive the cold winter weather to come, while the aphids themselves can't. In the spring these eggs will hatch into females only, who start giving birth again to girls only.

There are a few other types of animals that have only female offspring. It's a successful strategy for aphids because more offspring are born in a short time this way. Aphids have few defenses against predators and so they need large numbers of offspring to ensure that there are some survivors.

Say a mother aphid had ten children, half girls and half boys, and each girl had to mate with one of the males to have her own children. Then only five of that mother aphid's children would give birth to children of their own. Then imagine if a different aphid mother had ten children, *all females*, and those female children did not need to mate to have their own children. Then all ten of those children would give birth to children of their own. So the second aphid mother would have twice as many grandchildren as the first one.

Aphids are so tiny and squashable, they're easy to overlook. But though they look simple, they have one of the most complex and interesting life cycles of any insect. Just goes to show—you can't judge a bug by its cover!

SPITTLEBUGS

What They Look Like

The adult spittlebug is called a froghopper because it looks a little like a frog—a broad, squat, hopping creature, with longish legs and big eyes. It looks even more like another insect you might see hopping around on plants, a leafhopper, to whom it is closely related. But froghoppers are wider in back than front, while leafhoppers have parallel sides or taper in back. Adult froghoppers are ⅛ to ½ inch (4 to 10 mm) long, and can be brown, gray, or black. Like leafhoppers, they hop from plant to plant. Froghoppers have wings but seldom fly.

Where to Find Them

Most spittlebugs live on leafy weeds or grasses in fields or wooded areas. Sometimes a patch of weeds along a woodland trail can look like an army of men marched through, every one of them spitting as he passed. Spittlebugs also make their frothy nests on corn or strawberries, or other garden plants. I sometimes see them on trees.

The spittlebug nymph surrounds itself with a mass of froth that looks like a wad of spit on the stem of a plant or a blade of grass. About ⅛ inch (4 mm) long, the nymph is greenish or brownish and rather plain-looking. The oval-shaped body has no wings, no spines, and no spots. With its short legs, the nymph hangs onto the stem. The nymphs and adults live only in spring and summer, leaving eggs to survive over the winter protected by the frothy mass.

Class:
Insecta

Order:
Homoptera (homopterans)

Family:
Cercopidae (spittlebugs only)

Characteristics
The nymph is hidden in a frothy, spittlelike mass on plants. Adults are small, jumping insects, somewhat wider toward the back, and without the tall "knees" of grasshoppers and crickets.

Distribution:
Throughout the United States and Southern Canada.

Food:
Plant sap.

Froghopper
(adult spittlebug)

29

How to Catch Them

To catch a spittlebug, all you have to do is blow the froth away or gently push it away with your finger. It's not really spit, so it's okay to touch it. You can also squirt it away with water if you have a squirter handy, but don't squirt too hard or you might blow the bug away, too.

Inside you'll see a creature that's surprisingly small to have made such a mass. It clings to its twig, making no effort to move away. Don't try to pluck it off the twig. Spittlebug nymphs are clumsy and have a hard time grabbing a finger or a new twig. Their bodies are designed for holding on, not moving around. To take one home, put it and its twig in a jar with a damp paper towel or carry it in your hand.

Frothy Mass

How to Keep Them

Spittlebug nymphs and adults eat sap from live stems and leaves. So if you want to keep one as a pet, you'll need to dig up the plant it's on and move the plant to a flowerpot. Be careful to get as much of the roots as you can and keep them covered with soil at all times. Air will damage the roots. Once the plant is in the new pot, fill most of the extra space with soil, and water it at once. Leave the nymph where it is on the stem when you move the plant.

The nymph and its potted plant don't need to be in a container. The nymph won't move as long as the plant is healthy. Because adults hop from plant to plant, don't try keeping them as pets.

Throwing leaves or stems into a jar won't work for feeding a nymph because the sap no longer flows in a cut or uprooted plant. A spittlebug may live for a few days on an uprooted stem and may even make a new froth nest, but it won't last long. However, if you wish to keep a spittle-bug and its twig for a day or so, a jar with a slightly crumpled (not wadded), damp paper towel will do. Use a cloth lid, held in place with a rubber band.

What They Act Like

Can you imagine blowing enough bubbles with your body to fill up a large closet? Considering the size of a spittlebug, you can say that's exactly what it does. Does it blow the bubbles with its mouth? No, the bubbles come out of its back end! But it's still okay to touch them—they're not germy. The spittlelike froth is a combination of fluid from an opening in the rear of its body and a gluey substance from a gland.

The air to inflate the bubbles comes from the spittlebug's body, too. The spittlebug moves its tail up and down like a bellows, an accordion-like tool for blowing air on a fire. The nymph forces the air out through the fluid and glue mixture, creating bubbles one by one. The nymph's legs take hold of each bubble as it forms and move it forward, making room for the next. The little creature keeps at it until it is completely covered with bubbles for about a ½ inch (13 mm) in each direction.

The main reason they make the frothy mass is probably the same reason a woolly aphid covers itself with white woolly fluff, a leaf-rolling caterpillar wraps itself in a leaf, or a caddisfly larva makes a hollow tube to live in under water. All of these devices are hiding places from predators. It's true that the frothy mass is a lot easier to spot than the naked nymph, but many predators probably don't know there's a bug inside and won't look. Also, many of the animals that might bother to eat something as small as a froghopper, such as toads, frogs, lizards, and mantises, are not interested in items that aren't moving. They're programmed to recognize objects in motion as dinner. An interesting experiment would be to enclose some froth-covered spittlebugs and some bare spittlebugs with a predator and note which, if either, are eaten first.

Scientists have also suggested that the purpose of the froth is to keep the nymph's skin moist. This is a possibility. If the advantage were only in avoiding predators, then why don't adults also live in a frothy mass? Maybe because the adults need to be able to move about in order to find mates. Or maybe the adults' hopping, something the nymphs can't yet do, is a better way to escape predators. Part of the fun of being a scientist is coming up with possible explanations for behaviors you observe, and then finding a way to test your explanations.

Spittlebug Nymph Making Frothy Mass

PILLBUGS

What They Look Like

An unrolled pillbug looks like a little armored car tooling around. The legs underneath are barely visible as it scuttles from one hiding place to another. The gray plates of its back look like they could be metal. No head or tail is visible, just two tiny specks of eyes and two threadlike short antennae. The back is oval shaped, about ¼ to ½ inch (6 to 13 mm) long.

If you make your pillbugs a little home in a margarine tub, you'll soon see very tiny white "armored cars" in your tub. These babies—about the size of the head of a pin—are little copies of their parents. There is no larval stage, as there is with the caterpillar or mealworm. In fact, pillbugs aren't even true insects. Look at the legs. Insects have 6 legs and pillbugs have 14! Pillbugs are isopods, a type of crustacean. All isopods have 14 legs.

When you pick up a pillbug, its short, wiggly, white legs disappear and all that's left is a hard little ball. The pillbug turns into a little "pill." Not many animals can dispose of their legs and vulnerable soft tummies so handily. Looking closely, you can see the series of overlapping plates on the back of the pillbug. The plates spread out when it rolls up, so they can reach all the way around and cover the creature. (There's another animal that is in some ways similar to the pillbug. This mammal also has armor on its back and can roll into a ball. The pillbug family gets its scientific name, Armadillidiidae, from this animal—the armadillo.)

Where to Find Them

Pillbugs like dark, damp places, such as under rotting logs on the ground or under potted plants on a porch or sidewalk. They also like such places as the cracks between a concrete porch and the edge of a house. The small amount of soil and pieces of leaves in the cracks stay damp even in dry weather. You could also look under stones or rubber mats or garbage bags on the ground.

Pillbug

How to Catch Them

There's nothing to catching pill-bugs. Just pick them up and toss them into a jar with a damp, slightly crumpled paper towel. The only tricky part is making sure you really picked up a pill-bug. Sowbugs look a lot like pillbugs. They both have round-ed, gray armor plates across the back, and at first glance they are nearly identical.

Rolled-up Pillbug

The main difference is that sowbugs can't roll up. A pill-bug may not roll up right away, but if you try to make it form a ball with your fingers, it will. There is no way a sowbug can. The plates on its back aren't rounded enough.

Another difference is that sowbugs have little pointy "tails" and pill-bugs don't. Keeping pillbugs and sowbugs in the same container can be fun, but their behavior is not always the same.

How to Keep Them

Pillbugs and sowbugs can be kept for long periods in a big margarine con-tainer, on a layer of soil about 2 inches (5 cm) deep. Sand will do as well. Cover the container with a piece of wax paper with several small holes poked in it, and secure this lid with a rubber band. A cloth lid allows the

Class:	*Crustacea (crustaceans)*
Order:	*Isopoda (isopods)*
Family:	*Armadillidiidae (pillbugs only)*
Characteristics:	*Small and gray with an arched back of overlapping plates. They roll into a ball when disturbed.*
Distribution:	*Throughout the United States and parts of Canada.*
Food:	*Decaying plants and fungi.*

container to dry out too quickly. A plastic-wrap lid can hold in too much moisture, which makes mold grow inside. Wax paper is a good in-between.

When starting, add enough water to moisten the soil. After that, check the soil every week or so to make sure it's slightly damp, and add more water as needed. On top of the soil keep a handful or two of dead leaves, the crumbly rotting stuff you find on the ground in the woods. Pillbugs and sowbugs eat decaying leaves, so add new ones every other week or so. Add a raw potato slice every one to two weeks also. The animals can get moisture from it and will eat part of it. They also may eat pieces of over-ripe fruit or soft vegetables, lettuce, and tender stems and seedling roots.

To get your population going, you should probably start with at least 20 to 30 pillbugs. If you have fewer, give it a try; it may work. If the pill-bugs in your container get crowded after a while, crawling over one another, let some go under a log outdoors. Other pets may like to eat your extras. I've fed them to toads and scorpions.

What They Act Like

You may have been surprised to hear that pillbugs (and sowbugs) are not insects but crustaceans. Usually when we think of crustaceans we think of lobsters, crabs, shrimp, and other ocean creatures. Most crustaceans live in water or very near water. If most crustaceans have bodies suited for liv-ing in water, how do pillbugs survive on land?

Pillbugs have to protect their bodies from water loss by seeking out places that are cool and damp and avoiding hot dry places. They also must be careful about timing. The night air has more moisture in it, so pillbugs may become more active at night, leaving their daytime hiding places.

You can prove for yourself that pillbugs will choose a damp place over a dry place. Get a plastic tub or baking pan and put a damp paper towel in one half of it and a dry paper towel in the other half, and tape the tow-els together so nothing can crawl under them. Put a few pillbugs in the middle of the container and leave them for an hour. Where are they when you come back?

Here's another experiment you can try to see if they choose dark or light places. Cover half of a baking pan with black construction paper. Put some pillbugs in the pan, and put the pan under a lamp. After a few minutes, where are they?

Life in the water is much easier in some ways, biologically speaking. Our bodies are mostly water, and air has a very drying effect on our bod-ies. Animals (including us) lose water through the skin as sweat and in our wastes, and even through the air we breathe out, which is loaded with tiny water droplets. As humans we can always turn on the faucet or open the refrigerator for a drink to put water back into our bodies, but other animals can't. Dew is often the only water source for insects so their bodies are designed to save the water they already have.

Insects are very well protected against drying out. They have a waxy covering over their whole bodies that keeps water in. Insects breathe through small tubes that run throughout their bodies. The openings to these tubes can be closed off when the air outside is very hot and dry. These features of insects that enable them to survive in their natural environment are called **adaptations.** Pillbugs, being crustaceans, don't have these insect adaptations, so they hang out in damp, dark places and come out at night. This isn't all pillbugs do to keep their bodies from drying out. When conditions are very dry, pillbugs group together and make a pile. This behavior, called **bunching**, keeps them from losing so much water through their skins. Pillbugs may also roll themselves up to keep from losing water. A pillbug has a lunglike cavity on its underside that it uses for breathing. Rolling into a ball helps prevent water loss from this cavity.

What else might rolling up be good for? If a praying mantis tries to eat a pillbug, its mouthparts will just bounce off the hard plates of the pillbug. So the rolling up is a protection from the hungry jaws of predators. The rolling up not only helps us recognize them, but saves their lives in more ways than one.

MILLIPEDES

What They Look Like

It's important to be able to tell millipedes from centipedes because some centipedes can bite. The most noticeable difference is that millipedes have very short legs and move slowly. Centipedes have longer legs that get longer still toward the back end of the body. This keeps centipedes from stepping on their own "toes" as they run, and they are *fast*. If a millipede is as slow as a tortoise, then a centipede is as quick as a hare.

There are a number of other differences. Millipedes have two pairs of legs per body segment, while centipedes have one pair per segment. Centipedes have long antennae, millipedes have short ones; centipedes are flatter and wider, millipedes are more tubelike. And their walking is very different. Each millipede leg moves at the same time as its match on the other side of the body. This paired movement causes millipedes to glide along smoothly, as though flowing. In contrast, each centipede leg alternates movement with its match on the other side, causing the body to wriggle in an S-shape as it walks.

Although millipede means "1,000 feet," millipedes don't actually have 1,000 legs. But sometimes they have more than a hundred. If millipede means "1,000 feet," centipede must mean "100 feet," because there are 100 years in a century. A centipede may have dozens of legs, but none has exactly 100.

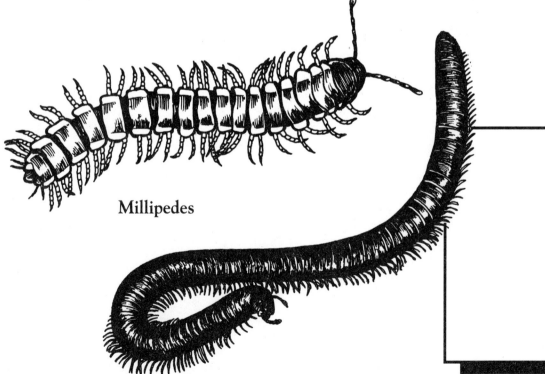

Millipedes

Where to Find Them

Lots of millipedes hang out under damp logs. I look for them in the same places I look for pillbugs—under the bark of logs, and under logs and rocks. (Remember to put the logs and rocks back where they were, for the benefit of the other creatures that live there.) Like pillbugs, millipedes are not true insects, as you might have

Millipedes on Leaves and Rotting Wood

guessed from their abundance of legs. (Insects have six.) They are in a class all to themselves, Diplopoda. They lack some of the adaptations that insects have for saving body moisture. Millipedes cope with this problem in some of the same ways pillbugs do (see the previous chapter).

How to Catch Them

Because their short legs are so slow, millipedes are easy to pick up. Centipedes are sometimes under logs, too, but are so much faster on their long legs they are almost impossible to catch. Since large centipedes may bite, don't even try to catch one. They're predators and have poison fangs for catching and killing prey. None in the United States or Canada could seriously hurt you, but the bite might be painful. Millipedes are vegetarians and don't bite.

Class: *Diplopoda (millipedes only)*

Characteristics: *Long bodies, usually cylinder-shaped, with dozens of legs. Two pairs of legs per body segment.*

Distribution: *Throughout the United States.*

Food: *Decaying plants.*

How to Keep Them

Millipedes are easy to raise in captivity. Keep them in the same kind of large margarine tub used for raising pillbugs. Put an inch or two of damp soil in the tub, then cover it with decaying leaves from the ground. Cover the container with wax paper with several small holes poked in it, and secure the paper with a rubber band. Keep the soil damp at all times.

Millipedes eat rotting leaves, or the roots or shoots of young plants. Some eat **fungi**, organisms that live in decaying matter. Try raw fruits, vegetables, and other plant parts to see what they like.

If you keep the tub moist and find a food they like, millipedes will probably reproduce in the tub. They might court, or try to interest one another in mating. The male will line up his body along the female's back. The tiny youngsters look just like their parents. The young shed their skins often as they grow and are white for a while afterward. This makes them easy to spot.

What They Act Like

Exposed millipedes will often *try* to run, but they're hopelessly slow. Some don't even try. Just as humans who are about to be struck will automatically cover their heads, a millipede does, too, by forming a tight coil, with the head in the center. If you hold a coiled millipede in the palm of your hand and leave it alone, it will soon uncoil and begin to glide across your hand and up your arm.

If a predator tries to bite a millipede, the millipede uses another means of defense: its stink glands. These glands, in rows along the body of some millipedes, give off a foul liquid when the millipede is bothered. The liquid not only stinks, but tastes awful,too. The **noxious** (physically harmful) smell is not bad enough for you to be concerned about; in fact, if you handle millipedes gently they probably won't smell at all. On a small one, the smell is not much. But a handful can be another matter. If you were to pick up about 20 millipedes at once, the smell might stay on your hand for a couple of days in spite of washing.

Some of the bigger and stinkier millipedes are brightly colored, like the black-and-yellow *Sigmouria*. A shrew or bird will remember the bad taste when it sees the bright colors again. Captive mantises, lizards, and toads usually won't eat millipedes. One bite and the mantis drops it. The toad spits it out. The hard slick skin of a millipede, made of **chitin**, can offer protection as well. Some predators just can't get a grip on it. Centipedes don't need these tricks because they have fangs and can run so fast.

Though these critters can be noxious, they are fun, too. Look down on a creeping millipede and notice the wavelike motion of the legs. The waves move from back to front! How many waves per second are there? Is the count always the same, or does it vary?

CLICK BEETLES

What They Look Like

There are many different species of click beetles, and they're all easily recognized by the snapping or clicking motion that causes them to leap. Most are ½ to 1 inch (13 to 25 mm) long. All have roughly the same shape, which is different from that of most other beetles. The sides of the click beetle are nearly parallel, and the back ends of the wings taper to a point. The **thorax**, or middle body part, has a distinct shape, too. The two back corners of a click beetle's squarish thorax are rather pointed, with the points aimed at the rear of the body.

One of the largest and most often seen click beetles is the Eyed Click Beetle, also called the Eyed Elater because the click beetle family is named Elateridae. The Eyed Click Beetle has two big fake eyes (actually black spots) on its thorax. The rest of its body looks like a mixture of salt and pepper. The fake eyes startle birds or snakes and give the click beetle a chance to escape predators that might eat it. Lots of butterflies and caterpillars have fake eyes for the same reason (see the Tiger Swallowtail in a later chapter).

Class:
Insecta

Order:
Coleoptera (beetles)

Family:
Elateridae (click beetles only)

Characteristics:
Long and narrow body with parallel sides, somewhat flattened. Jumps straight up with a clicking sound. Larvae are worm-shaped and hard-bodied.

Distribution:
Throughout the United States. The Eyed Click Beetle can be found throughout the eastern and southern states.

Food:
Larvae usually feed on roots and seeds. Some adults eat flowers and leaves. Others don't eat at all.

Eyed Click Beetle

The larvae of click beetles are such major pests to gardeners and farmers that they have their own name—wireworms. Wireworms are worm-shaped with shiny, shell-like skin. They can be yellow, gray, or reddish brown. Except for the color and hard, shiny skin, they resemble earthworms.

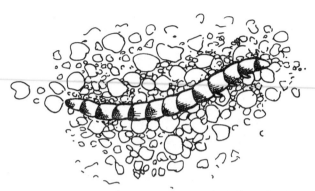

Wireworm—Larva of Click Beetle

You probably haven't thought of beetles as insects that leap. It's true that most beetles don't. The click beetle leaps in a completely different way than grasshoppers and crickets, which use their legs. The click beetle uses its body to leap.

When a falcon is diving through the air to capture another bird, it can go faster than 180 miles an hour (290 kmph). It's the fastest animal on earth. The falcon is a majestic bird, and it seems proper that it should hold such an honor. And next to the falcon on the platform of champions is the small and humble click beetle. Not an awe-inspiring creature like the falcon, but a world record holder nonetheless. The plain little click beetle can **accelerate**, or gain speed, faster than all the other leaping animals of the world. So the fastest accelerator goes from a standstill to a fast speed more quickly than any other leaper. (In cars, the fastest accelerator would be the one to go from a stop to a speed of 60 miles per hour, or 97 kmph, in the fewest number of seconds.)

Where to Find Them

Adult click beetles are usually found on the flowers and leaves of trees and bushes. Some species live in rotting logs or under dead bark. Most adult click beetles eat leaves but do little damage.

Female adults lay their eggs in the soil in spring. After hatching, the larvae, or wireworms, spread out and stay underground, like earthworms. Some wireworms remain worms for up to six years before turning into adults! Wireworms eat roots, underground stems, and bulbs. They'll eat the roots of almost any garden plant. Sometimes they make tunnels through potatoes, carrots, beets, and onions, all of which grow underground. So don't bite into a carrot or other vegetable if you see a small tunnel in it. A wireworm may be in your next bite!

How to Catch Them

Since adult click beetles live mostly in trees and shrubs, they can be collected by sweeping a net through the leaves. You may sometimes find them indoors or on patios. They don't bite or sting and can be picked up easily.

How to Keep Them

If you find a click beetle, keep it in a small terrarium—4 × 7 inches (10 × 18 cm) or larger—or a jar with a cloth lid held in place with a rubber band. Keep a loosely crumpled, damp paper towel with it, or a fresh slice of raw potato, for moisture. You can keep several beetles together; they won't hurt each other. Try offering fresh leaves of the tree or shrub nearest to where you found it. Be sure the leaves are still on the twig, and place it in a cup or vase of water to keep it fresh.

For wireworm pets, collect some of the soil in which you found them to put in their container. Use enough soil so that it is at least 3 inches (8 cm) deep. Feed wireworms chunks of root vegetables such as potatoes, turnips, and carrots.

What They Act Like

People have argued for years about how and why the click beetle leaps. The action is so fast, it's hard to tell exactly what's happening. Everyone agrees, at least, about what parts of its body are used to make it leap. Just above the waist, on its belly, the beetle has a peglike spine sticking out. The peg is shaped like the horn of a western saddle, the knob that sticks up in front of a rider on a horse. When the click beetle bends at the waist, the peg fits very tightly into a groove below the waist, much in the same way two popbeads fit together. The beetle has to push very hard with a strong muscle to make the peg go in. Some scientists think the popping of the peg into the groove is what makes the beetle leap. Others think pulling the peg *out* of the groove causes a sudden snap. The click beetle's ability to flex or bend its body in the middle, just as people can bend at the waist, sets this beetle apart from most insects.

One reason click beetles leap may be to turn themselves over. When a click beetle is on its back, it bends at the waist, so that its head and "tail" rise while the middle of its back stays on the table or ground. The sudden thrust of the peg into the groove makes the click beetle's back **recoil**, or be pushed hard against the ground, sending the click beetle flying into the air. In the air it turns a half circle, reaching a height of about 12 inches (30 cm). The beetle lands on its feet about 75 percent of the time. If not, it leaps again. The name of the click beetle comes from the fact that this motion makes a clicking noise.

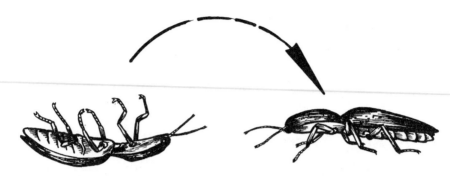

Click Beetle Flipping Itself onto Its Feet

This may not be the only explanation for why click beetles leap. Although many beetles have trouble turning themselves over when they end up on their backs, some species of click beetles can actually turn themselves over easily *without* clicking. They can turn over by spreading their wings. And here's another thing to consider: click beetles sometimes leap from a belly-*down* position.

Why else might an animal leap? Frogs and toads leap partly to get around, partly to escape from predators. Have you ever tried to catch a frog or toad? It's not easy! Leaping might make the beetles harder to catch, but click beetles often don't leap when you move to pick them up. They often play dead instead. They seem to be easy prey for a predator.

Maybe the playing-dead act and the click work together to help the beetle escape predators. Some predators, like toads and preying mantises, will snap up most moving insects but totally ignore still ones. And most predators have short attention spans—they won't watch for long. So a predator might turn away from a beetle that seems dead, giving the beetle a chance to pull its second trick—a click, a leap, a twist in midair, and a graceful landing out of reach. No lunch here for the toad or bird or mantis, not this time. Does your click beetle leap when you try to pick it up? Or does it play dead—and *then* leap?

The click beetle is full of mystery. We don't know positively how or why it snaps into the air. If you grow up to be a biologist, you might spend years answering questions like these by testing the beetles' reactions to different situations. Biologists have fun unraveling such mysteries as the click of the click beetle.

DADDY-LONG-LEGS OR HARVESTMEN

What They Look Like

Daddy-long-legs, or harvestmen, are most easily recognized by their very long and very thin legs, which look a lot like the legs of a crane fly. Crane flies are also called daddy-long-legs in some parts of the country, but crane flies have wings, only six legs, and long thin bodies, so the two are easy to tell apart.

The body of the daddy-long-legs is only ¼ to ⅓ inch (6 to 8 mm) long, but the legs are 2 to 4 inches (5 to 10 cm) long. With legs stretched out, the daddy-long-legs may be 8 inches (20 cm) across! Some have two obvious joints in each leg, that look as though they're covered by black wrap-around knee pads or sweatbands. Below the last joint, the legs bend as a thin fishing pole does when it has a big fish on the line, but in the opposite direction.

Although the legs are long, daddy-long-legs walk with their bodies close to the ground, and the middle part of the legs high in the air. My pet daddy-long-legs has a rust colored body, light brown legs with black joints, and rust-colored claws by its mouth, which can be folded up or stretched out. The eyes on this species are black specks, about one-fourth of the way back on the body. On some species, the eyes sit up on stalks, looking

Class:
Arachnida (spiders, mites, and their kin)

Order:
Opiliones or Phalangida (daddy-long-legs or harvestmen only)

Characteristics:
Eight thread-like long legs and a short, round body held near the ground.

Distribution:
Throughout North America.

Food:
Mainly living insects; sometimes dead animals or plant juices.

Daddy-long-legs (Legs are often broken off.)

out to each side. Other species come in different colors. Males are more brightly colored.

Although daddy-long-legs are related to spiders, having eight legs as spiders do, there are a number of differences. The two main body parts of spiders are easy to distinguish, but the head and body of a daddy-long-legs appear to be joined together into a single egg-shaped unit. Spiders generally have six to eight eyes, while daddy-long-legs have only two tiny eyes. Spiders have poison fangs for killing their prey, and silk for making shelters, traps, or webs. Daddy-long-legs have only a pair of claws by the mouth, no fangs, and they make no traps or webs. The eggs of spiders often hatch in the autumn, but daddy-long-legs eggs wait until spring.

When I was in elementary school I used to ride my bike to school every day. Children were not allowed in the building until just before time for school to begin, so we waited outside. Every morning in autumn there were dozens of daddy-long-legs on the brick walls of the building. The boys used to pluck them off the walls by their long legs and fling them at the girls. Most of the girls screamed and ran, which of course just brought on more flinging. I thought the girls were silly and the boys sillier—I worried about the poor daddy-long-legs, many of whom lost their legs or their lives.

Where to Find Them

Daddy-long-legs can be seen on walls or hanging upside down under deck-railings, or under decks, and similar structures, where they're easily spotted. They usually hide during the day, but often not very well. At night they wander around in search of food. These creatures are most common in late summer or autumn—harvest time— which is why they're often called "harvestmen."

How to Catch Them

The safest way to catch a daddy-long-legs is to let it step onto your hand, then cup your other hand around it until you get it into a container. Remember, they have no poison fangs and no jaws, so they can't bite. Although their long legs appear to make them easy to pick up, if you're not gentle you may pull a leg off.

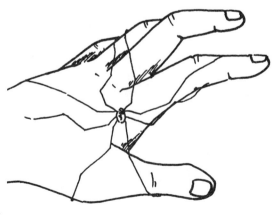

Catching a Daddy-long-legs

How to Keep Them

Daddy-long-legs will be all right for a couple of days in a jar with a damp paper towel for moisture. Cover the jar with cloth, secured with a rubber band. I've never had one eat in a jar, although they will eat in a terrarium. A daddy-long-legs can live in a terrarium with a small lizard. Lizards are predators, but many don't eat daddy-long-legs, perhaps because they don't like the long legs. The daddy-long-legs will eats the lizard's leftovers. If the lizard leaves a small piece of a moth on the terrarium floor, the daddy-long-legs will find it and eat it where it lies.

You can try other foods than dead insects. Some eat small live insects that they tear apart with their claws. Try aphids, which can be found on garden plants. Some eat soft fruits and vegetables from which they squeeze juice with their claws.

What They Act Like

The second pair of legs, twice as long as any of the others, are used to detect danger. They actually work as feelers. When the daddy-long-legs is disturbed, these longer legs feel around in the air.

These special legs need special care, and they get it. The daddy-long-legs cleans the second pair of legs by pulling them one at a time through the mouthparts, all the way to the tips. The other legs are cleaned too, but not as often.

The legs have another interesting feature aside from being used as feelers. When a leg is pulled off, it twitches, attracting the attention of a predator and letting the daddy-long-legs escape.

Daddy-long-legs usually die in autumn, except in places that are warm year-round. But before they do, they mate. The female lays eggs in the ground, under rocks, or in cracks in wood. She has a long egg-depositing tube that comes out of her body when needed. When they hatch, they crawl to the surface of the ground and shed their skins, leaving them all white for a short while. The young use their second pair of legs as feelers, just as the adults do. They stay hidden while tiny, coming out in the open more by midsummer. Then they may join the adults wandering about at night, or gathering on the walls of buildings.

If you find a daddy-long-legs on an early school morning in autumn, here are some questions to keep you busy: Can you get one to raise its second pair of legs? Does touching its leg work? Touching its body? How does it react if you blow on it gently? What if you lay a hand in its path? Try moving your hand above it but not touching it. Does it see well enough to respond? Does the daddy-long-legs ever raise both second legs at once, or only one at a time? Does it favor right or left? And if your friends get the urge to fling a daddy-long-legs, tell them it might be more fun to watch.

BUGS THAT LOOK LIKE SOMETHING THEY'RE NOT

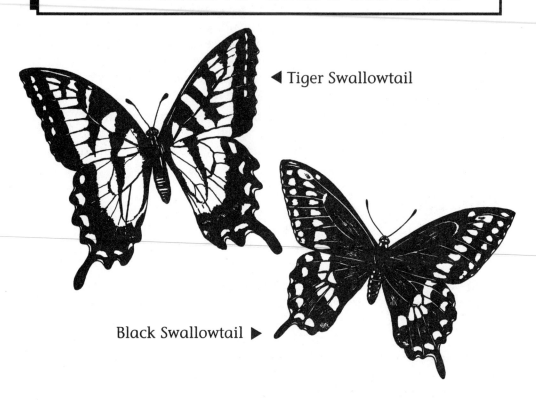

◀ Tiger Swallowtail

Black Swallowtail ▶

▲ Monarch

TIGER SWALLOWTAILS

What They Look Like

There are lots of swallowtail species in the United States. Almost all swallowtail butterflies have a long "tail" off the back end of each back wing. The tail looks somewhat like that of a swallow, a bird that sometimes has a forked tail. The wings are mostly yellow. You can be sure it's a Tiger Swallowtail if you see black tiger stripes. Each stripe starts at the front edge of one front wing and moves back toward the tail. Both front and back wings on each side have black outer edges with blue and red dots on the black part. The wingspan of the adult is about 5½ inches (14 cm), making it one of the biggest butterflies.

The eggs of the Tiger Swallowtail are tiny, round, and yellow-green. The mother lays only one or two per tree, on the undersides of leaves. She lays about 200 in all, so she has a lot of traveling to do! Tiny caterpillars hatch from the eggs. (The familiar word *caterpillar* is another name for the larva

Tiger Swallowtail

Class: *Insecta*

Order: *Lepidoptera (butterflies and moths)*

Family: *Papilionidae (swallowtails)*

Genus and species of Eastern Tiger Swallowtail: Papilio glaucus

Genus and species of Western Tiger Swallowtail: P. rutulus

Characteristics: *Wingspan up to 5½ inches (14 cm). Wings yellow with black borders; black stripes running back from front edge of wings. Larvae green, larger at head end, with fake eyes on back of head area.*

Distribution: *Eastern Tiger Swallowtail found over eastern two-thirds of United States east of the Rocky Mountains; Western Tiger Swallowtail over western one-third of United States.*

Food: *Adults eat flower nectar. Eastern Tiger Swallowtail larvae eat mostly leaves of cherry and tulip trees. Western Tiger Swallowtail larvae feed on leaves of willow, poplar, and hops.*

of a butterfly or moth.) At first these little larvae are dark brown or black, with
a white saddle-shaped marking across
the back. As they get bigger they become
green, with two narrow stripes across the
body, one yellow and one black, behind
the fake eyes. The head end is much
larger than the tail end. When full
grown the caterpillar is about 1½ inches
(4 cm) long.

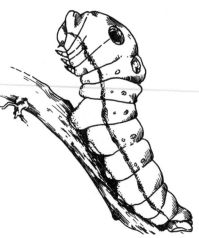

**Caterpillar of Tiger
Swallowtail**

If a hungry robin spots this plump
green caterpillar moving along the
branch, the bird may think it has found
a meal. But lunch could take a nasty
turn. The caterpillar may rear back,
showing what looks like two huge eyes
and an orange forked tongue. If this happens, the robin will zoom away,
thinking it has found a snake.

The caterpillar tricked the robin. What the bird actually saw were not
eyes, but two big orange spots on the back of the caterpillar, each with a
black center that looks like the **pupil**, or black opening in the center of an
eye. Its real eyes are tiny and on the front of its head. The "forked tongue"
that spooked the robin was really two orange horns that usually stay
inside the head, but pop out when the caterpillar is upset.

Where to Find Them

Adult swallowtails often gather around puddles to sip the moisture and
salts in the water, so an area with lots of puddles is a good place to look.
Look also for activity around their favorite flowers—clover, daylilies, aza-
leas, butterfly bush, butterfly weed, and glossy abelia. Adults suck up
nectar, a sugary substance produced by these flowers, during the day
with their long strawlike mouthparts. Their favorite leaves for egg laying
are those of cherry trees and tulip trees. The leaves of ash, peach, apple,
catalpa, hornbeam, cottonwood, and sassafras trees are acceptable for
eggs as well. After the larvae or caterpillars hatch, they feed on the leaves
of these trees at night, resting or hiding during the day. Swallowtails are
active from April to November, for a shorter period in the colder states.

When fully grown, the larvae leave the tree and find a sheltered spot
to **pupate**, or turn into a butterfly. Using the silk gland next to its mouth,
the larva fixes a silken loop around its back and anchors it to a fixed surface. The loop supports it as it wiggles out of its skin. Under the skin is a
chrysalis, sort of like the cocoon of a moth. But while cocoons are made
of silk threads, a chrysalis is covered by hardened skin. The chrysalis

spends the winter enclosed in its new, hard, brown skin. Inside, the cater-pillar turns into a butterfly, a process called metamorphosis. In the spring, the chrysalis splits, and out comes the new butterfly.

How to Catch Them

The caterpillars can be handled easily and will gladly crawl up and down your arm. Some caterpillars have spines that can sting, so before you pick one up, be sure it matches the description of one of the safe ones in this book. The Introduction has a list of other insects not to pick up.

If you find an adult Tiger Swallowtail that has just crawled out of its chrysalis, you may be able to hold it briefly. Gently slip your finger between its body and the stem or leaf it's perched on. It will transfer its legs one by one from stem to finger. Move very slowly to help the butter-fly keep its balance, because it can't fly yet. You might feel it trembling as it pumps fluid into its wings to straighten and harden them. *Don't touch the wings!* They are damaged easily at this point.

It may fly from your finger. If not, leave the butterfly in a place it can easily fly from when its wings are ready, which will be about an hour after emerging. A butterfly net will be needed to catch older adults. Be very careful not to tear or rub scales from their wings.

Tiger Swallowtail—From Chrysalis to Butterfly

How to Keep Them

To keep Tiger Swallowtail larvae, provide them with fresh leaves of the tree on which you found them. The leaves should be on a twig, with the end in water. Provide fresh leaves daily. When grown, a larva may make its chrysalis in a terrarium if you provide a rough vertical surface for it to hang from—a brick maybe.

Watching a new butterfly emerge from its chrysalis is a thrill, but it doesn't take long, so you'll miss it if you don't keep an eye on the chrysalis. After the new wings have hardened, adults will probably be damaged by captivity, so don't try to keep them. Let newly emerged butterflies outside as soon as you can. Fluttering against the sides of a container is not good for their wings.

What They Act Like

You've already seen one of the gimmicks Tiger Swallowtails use for avoiding predators—rearing up with fake eyes and horns to look like a snake. Tiger swallowtails have a couple of other ways to keep from being eaten. One is hiding during the day. The caterpillar produces a thread of silk with the **silk glands**, enclosed in **spinnerets** near its mouth, making a tight silk platform on a leaf. The silk pulls the edges of the leaf up and partly over the platform, where the caterpillar rests until night, when it's time to feed.

Another way Tiger Swallowtails avoid predators is by imitating the looks of the Pipevine Swallowtail, a brown butterfly species that tastes bad. The Pipevine Swallowtail eats a plant called pipevine, which has a bad-tasting chemical that builds up in the body of the Pipevine Swallowtail, making it taste bad, too. Predators learn to avoid eating it. In the South, where the Pipevine Swallowtail is common, about half of the Tiger Swallowtails are brown, so that they look like the Pipevine Swallowtail. Predators, such as birds, mistake the Tiger for the bad-tasting Pipevine Swallowtail and leave it alone.

This strategy—imitating the looks or behavior of another plant or animal in order to protect itself from predators or in some other way increase its chance of survival—is called **mimicry**. The fake eyes of the Tiger Swallowtail caterpillar are a form of mimicry. Fake eye spots can be found in many other unrelated animals. You learned in an earlier chapter that the Eyed Click Beetle has two fake eyes on its back. The Polyphemus Moth has fake eyes on its wings, which it can flash open suddenly when disturbed. Even animals with backbones use this strategy. A fish with a fake eye near the tail has a better chance of survival because a predator may dive for the wrong end, while the fish darts the other way. The Four-eye Butterfly Fish is one such trickster.

This trickery isn't confined to insects or even to animals. Salamanders may also be mimics of other salamanders that taste bad. One such salamander has the scientific name *Desmognathus imitator*. Some flowers have parts that mimic insects, to attract other insects that may pollinate the flowers. A successful strategy may turn up again and again in the animal world. How many more mimics have we yet to discover?

BLACK SWALLOWTAILS

What They Look Like

The adults of both the eastern and western species of Black Swallowtail look alike—both males and females are mostly black, with the same "tail" on the back wing as other swallowtails have. The tail is a long fingerlike projection pointing backward off the rear of the hind wings. There are two rows of yellow spots along the outer edge of each wing. On the hind wing only is a row of blue spots and a single red spot. Black Swallowtails are smaller than their cousins, the 5½-inch (14-cm) Tiger Swallowtails, with a wingspan of only 3½ inches (9 cm). Still, pretty big! The Eastern Black Swallowtail is a common species in the eastern two-thirds of the United States and southern Canada, with a western counterpart called the Western Black Swallowtail or Baird's Swallowtail.

The larva (caterpillar) of both eastern and western species is at first dark with a white saddle mark on its back.

Black Swallowtail
(male)

Class: *Insecta*

Order: *Lepidoptera (butterflies and moths)*

Family: *Papilionidae (swallowtails)*

Genus and species of Eastern Black Swallowtail: Papilio polyxenes asterius

Genus and species of Western Black Swallowtail: P. bairdii

Characteristics: *Wingspan up to 3½ inches (9 cm). Mostly black, with two rows of yellow spots along the outer edge of each wing; a row of blue spots and a single red spot on each hind wing. Larvae mostly green with black crossbands; yellow dots on black bands.*

Distribution: *Eastern Black Swallowtail is found over the eastern two-thirds of the United States and in southern Canada east of the Rockies. Western Black Swallowtail occurs in the southwestern corner of the United States.*

Food: *Adults eat flower nectar. Larva of Eastern Black Swallowtail eats leaves of carrot, parsley, celery, and parsnip plants. Larva of Western Black Swallowtail eats sagebrush (Artemesia).*

The older larva is mostly green with black crossbands. On each crossband are several yellow dots. It does not have the fake eyes of the Tiger Swallowtail larva. Larvae of the eastern and western species have different diets.

Larva of Black Swallowtail

Where to Find Them

The Eastern Black Swallowtail larva eats common garden plants—the greens of carrots and the herbs parsley, fennel, and dill—so the Black Swallowtail may be easier to attract than the Tiger Swallowtail. (If you want to try planting a butterfly garden, you can get seeds for all of these at a hardware store or plant nursery in the spring.) Adult Black Swallowtails will be attracted to your garden to lay their eggs on these plants. When the eggs hatch, the larvae will eat the carrot greens and the herbs, so if you want some, too, plant enough for both you and the larvae.

The larvae of the western variety eat sagebrush. The adults, like most adult butterflies, feed on nectar. So you can attract adults by planting trees and flowers that provide nectar, such as apple and peach trees, lantana, thoroughwort, butterfly weed, Indian blanket, New England aster, phlox, purple loosestrife, various thistles, and zinnias.

How to Catch Them

Adults can't hurt you, but should be handled with great care because their wings can be easily damaged. If they will sit on your hand or climb up your arm, consider yourself lucky, but never touch their wings. The first butterfly I ever saw come out of its chrysalis was a Black Swallowtail. It crawled to the top of the plant from which its chrysalis hung, and sat very still for what seemed like a long time. I was amazed that it let me get so close and photograph its beautiful new wings. I could easily have picked it up. I realized finally that it *couldn't* fly because its wings weren't hardened yet.

The larvae will crawl happily up and down your arm and will not sting. A few caterpillars will sting, so be sure it fits the description of one of the safe ones in the book before you pick it up. In the Introduction is a list of other bugs not to pick up.

How to Keep Them

The larvae will grow well in captivity as long as you provide fresh leaves daily of carrot, parsley, dill, or fennel, or any other plant you may find them on (sagebrush for the western species). They don't move around other than crawling to the next leaf, so any container big enough to hold a freshly cut bunch of leaves will do, such as a large jar (quart size or bigger) for up to three or four caterpillars. A cloth lid held in place with a rubber band allows fresh air to circulate.

The leaves will last longer if you put the ends of the stems in a small cup of water. But if you supply fresh leaves every day, they don't have to be in water. The little beasts themselves don't need water as long as they have fresh leaves daily. Well-fed caterpillars generate a lot of feces, or bodily waste—called **fras**—which must be dumped out frequently. Those that live in a dirty cage are more likely to catch diseases.

When the caterpillars get over 1 inch (25 mm) long, move them to a terrarium big enough to hold a many-branched stick. You can tape a rectangle of cloth tightly over the top. The caterpillars will need the stick to hang from as they form their chrysalises. If you keep a chrysalis indoors, check it often. As soon as the adult comes out, gently carry the whole branch outdoors so that the adult can fly away as soon as it is able.

What They Act Like

Black Swallowtail Chasing Frisbee

Just as some Tiger Swallowtails look like, or mimic, the bad-tasting Pipevine Swallowtail, Black Swallowtail females do, too. This provides them some safety from predators who may have learned to avoid the bad-tasting Pipevine Swallowtail.

Have you ever seen a butterfly chase a Frisbee? Many will fly at any object that moves past them. Are they trying to play? No, they're males looking for females. A male finds a perch where he watches for females and flies out to inspect anything that goes by. Every two or three days he finds a new perch. Or instead of perching, he may patrol the area by flying around. Males often follow trails or roads, so if you sit by a path in the woods, you may see the same one pass you three times in a half hour, going the same direction each time.

The female flies to a hilltop to mate, with the male following. They flutter near one another, as a courtship greeting. Then they land and mate. A female may live no longer than a week, and if she does, she may mate more than once.

After mating she slowly flutters near the parsley or carrot leaves, then lands and tastes the leaves with her feet. (Yes, a butterfly's sense of taste is in its feet!) If it's the right plant, she curls her abdomen down and leaves a single creamy yellow egg, then flies off to lay another.

MONARCHS

What They Look Like

The wings of the beautiful Monarch butterfly are mostly orange, with black borders and a network of black veins through the orange. Along the black borders are white dots. The body is black, with white dots on the thorax. The Monarch uses only four of its legs. The front two are useless and are held folded up against the body. With a 3½-inch (9-cm) wingspan, the Monarch is one of the largest butterflies in the United States and Canada, although not as big as some of the swallowtails.

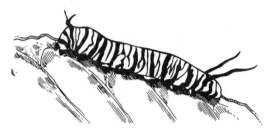

The Monarch caterpillar, as it grows, develops yellow, black, and white rings around its body. Its final length is about 2 inches (5 cm).

Monarch Caterpillar

Where to Find Them

The caterpillars of Monarchs eat only milkweed plants, which is why Monarchs are also called milkweed butterflies. The adults lay their eggs on milkweed, so your key to finding larvae or adults is finding the plant. Milkweed grows in abandoned lots or on roadsides—it's a tall, common weed. Some people transplant the weed to their yards to attract Monarchs.

There are over 100 species of milkweed in North America. One thing they all have in common is

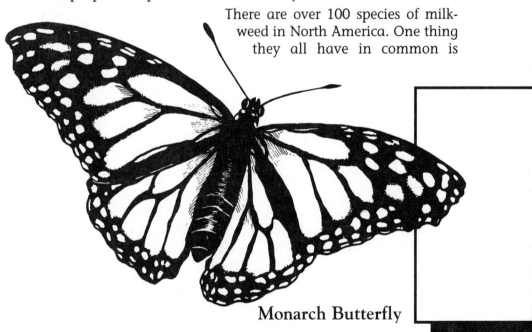

Monarch Butterfly

54

milky sap. If you snap a twig on a milkweed plant, the sap that bleeds out looks like thick white milk. Common milkweed has smooth, thick, waxy leaves, rose-colored or greenish white flowers, and special cone-shaped cases that hold the seeds. These cases eventually break open and release the seeds, which are carried in the air by distinctive white feathery fluff attached to the seeds.

Adult Monarchs spend their winters in the southern United States or Mexico and their summers in Canada, so people in the states in between see them only when they stop to lay eggs or feed on flower nectar during their journey. For example, in North Carolina they pass through in April or May on their way north and again in September on their way south, but this varies in other parts of the country. You may want to check with a local science museum to see when they pass through your area.

The larvae hatch from the eggs about three days after the eggs are laid, and the tiny larvae begin eating milkweed leaves. In about two weeks, the larvae are full grown.

How to Catch Them

You don't want to touch any eggs or very small caterpillars, because they're easily killed. Larger caterpillars can be handled easily. They'll happily crawl over your skin, tickling as they go. You may want to leave your new friends outdoors and visit them often. They won't go very far until they're adults.

If you decide to bring them home, bring the milkweed twigs too. Place the cut end of the milkweed in a cup of water. (Cut the end with scissors

Class:	*Insecta*
Order:	*Lepidoptera (butterflies and moths)*
Family:	*Danaidae (milkweed butterflies)*
Genus and species:	Danaus plexippus
Characteristics:	*Wings mostly orange, with black borders, and black veins across the orange; white dots along the black borders. Larva has yellow, black, and white rings around the body.*
Distribution:	*Throughout the United States, as well as Mexico in winter and Canada in summer.*
Food:	*Adults feed on flower nectar. Larvae eat leaves of milkweed and related plants.*

to help it soak up water.) Put cup and twig with eggs or caterpillars into a terrarium with a mesh or cloth lid.

A few species of caterpillars can sting, so before you touch one be sure that it matches the description of a safe one in this book. The Introduction has a list of other bugs not to touch.

How to Keep Them

Captive Monarch caterpillars need a steady supply of fresh milkweed to eat. When they reach about 2 inches (5 cm) in length, they're through eating. They become restless then and crawl around for about half a day, looking for a horizontal (sideways) stem that will hold a chrysalis. You may want to move them to a stick that has some horizontal branches. If you can get the stick to stand up in a pan of water, (try using a big wad of modeling clay or a spiky stem supporter from a florist) the water will keep the caterpillars from escaping. Then you can take them out of the terrarium so you can watch the miraculous thing that's going to happen.

The caterpillar, using the spinneret at its mouth, makes a lump of silk on a branch and attaches its tail end to the lump. It then hangs upside down from the lump in a J or fishhook position for about 24 hours. Then the skin splits at the back of the head, is pushed up toward the tail, and falls away. Slowly its new skin underneath hardens and turns a beautiful light green with a design of shiny gold dots that look like little golden nails. It no longer looks like a caterpillar, but like a little case. This is the chrysalis.

Chrysalis of Monarch

After one to three weeks, the chrysalis becomes almost clear, and the orange and black wings of the developing butterfly are visible. This means the butterfly will be coming out soon. It comes out very quickly, so it's time to take your friend outdoors unless you plan to watch it constantly. Just after the butterfly emerges from the chrysalis, its body is full of fluid which it pumps into the crumpled wings, causing them to straighten out. The new Monarch butterfly will let go of any extra fluid, so put a cloth under it if you still have it indoors. When the wings dry and harden—about two hours after emerging—the butterfly is ready to fly away. At this time, if you want to, you may try gently to put your finger under the butterfly's legs, but move slowly because it can't balance well yet. Don't touch the wings, or you may damage them permanently.

What They Act Like

To protect themselves from predators, Monarchs eat milkweed, which has chemicals in it that make the Monarch taste bad. Animals that eat Monarchs usually throw up. The bright wing pattern helps predators remember the Monarch and avoid eating another one. Monarchs also have a famous mimic—a butterfly called the Viceroy. The Viceroy looks almost exactly like the Monarch except for one little black line across each hind wing. The chapter on Tiger Swallowtails can give you some ideas why.

For years scientists have assumed that the Viceroy has a bland taste and that predators avoid it because of its resemblance to the Monarch. However, recent research has suggested that the Viceroy may have a bad taste, too. This mimicry is not the kind where the original tastes bad and the mimic tastes good, which is called **Batesian mimicry** after Henry Bates, the nineteenth-century English naturalist who first described it. Instead it may be the kind of mimicry where both original and mimic taste bad, called **Mullerian mimicry**, after Fritz Muller, a nineteenth-century Brazilian zoologist who first worked it out. Mullerian mimicry actually works better because the predator gets the negative message every time it eats the pattern in question, not just half the time.

Mimicry is not so uncommon in insects. However, Monarchs do something no other butterfly does. They **migrate**, or travel each year from one region or climate to another for feeding and breeding. In autumn they migrate southward in huge groups, going to the same places every year—certain groups of trees in Mexico, California, and Florida. One small area in Mexico gets tens of millions of Monarchs every winter—lucky people who live nearby!

Migrating Monarch Butterflies

As you might have guessed, Monarch butterfiles migrate to avoid the cold winter, which can kill insects. Other butterflies die in autumn, leaving either eggs or chrysalises to spend the winter in a sort of **hibernation**, or deep sleep. How did Monarchs develop such a different strategy? Monarchs first appeared thousands of years ago in Mexico, where it's warm year-round. Because it was warm, they did not need a period of hibernation as part of their life cycle. At that time there was no milkweed in the United States or Canada, where it was too cold. Gradually the climate warmed and milkweed spread into the United States, followed by Monarchs. Here they encountered cold winters for the first time. Their response was to head back to their homeland for the winter—a unique solution to the problem of freezing weather.

As milkweed moved farther and farther north with the warming climate, the Monarchs followed, and the length of their migration became greater and greater. The 2,000-mile one-way trip that some Monarchs make today is a result of that gradual increase in distance. And two thousand miles is a *long way* for even a bird to travel, but for an insect, it's almost unbelievable.

To track the migration of Monarch butterflies, researchers in Canada work with people from all over North America who raise the butterflies. A tag is placed on each butterfly. The tag, made just for Monarchs, has a special glue on it that holds it onto the front wing. Scientists worked hard to come up with a tag that would stay on but not hurt butterflies or keep them from flying.

Each tag comes with an identification number on it. It also bears, in tiny print, the address of the researcher in Canada who runs the tagging program and who sends tags to the people who raise Monarchs. When a tagged butterfly is released, the person who tagged it records the tag number, date, and location. This information is sent to the researcher in Canada for his or her files. If someone finds the butterfly later, the information on the tag enables him or her to notify the researcher.

How do the Monarchs know to go to the same spot every winter? This is a puzzling question, because the Monarchs that migrate to Mexico in autumn are the children of those that flew north through the United States to Canada in spring. Their parents could not have taught them, because their parents died before they were born. We know that they use the sun to help them maintain a steady course, but we don't know how they start out in the right direction. Maybe you'll be the one to figure out this insect mystery.

BUGS THAT LIVE AND WORK IN GROUPS

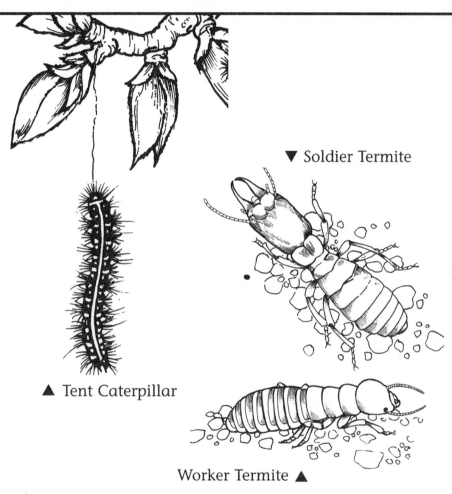

▲ Tent Caterpillar

▼ Soldier Termite

Worker Termite ▲

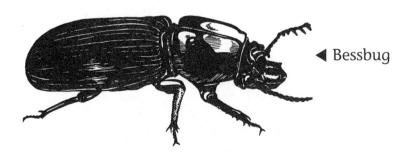

◄ Bessbug

TERMITES

What They Look Like

Termites are related to ants and look something like them. But termites are usually white and they don't have the skinny waist of an ant. And while ants have a hard exoskeleton, termites are soft-bodied. The worker and soldier termites are about as long as a new pencil eraser on a standard pencil—about ³⁄₁₆ inch (5 mm). The soldier has a large head and jaws. The queen termite is much bigger than the workers, soldiers, and king. (The jobs of the worker, soldier, queen, and king are described later, in "What They Act Like.")

Imagine climbing into the bathtub or sitting down on the toilet and suddenly crashing right through the bathroom floor into your basement—tub or toilet, too! This has happened to some people because of termites. Termites eat wood, and most houses are built with wooden frames. The supports under the floors and behind the walls are wood. Termites can get inside the wood and hollow it out so that it looks okay from the outside, but it's weak as a straw. Then one day, crash! It's amazing that something so weak-looking can do so much damage. Don't worry, though—most people have their houses sprayed with chemicals every few years to keep the termites out.

Termites can be pesky all right, but they do have their good points. They are commonly found in nature, in the woods, where they are not pests, but just part of the natural **ecosystem**, which includes all of the living and nonliving things

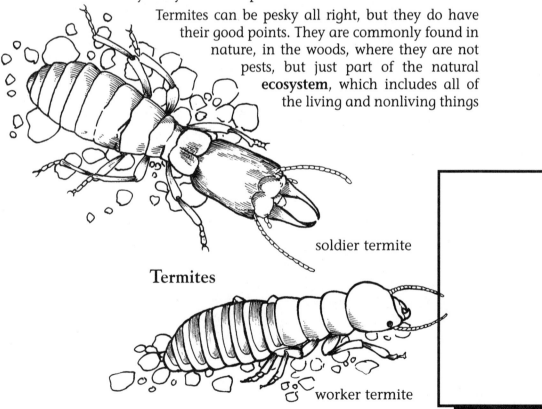

Termites

soldier termite

worker termite

60

that interact with each other, depend on each other, and function as a unit. Termites never attack or kill living trees, only rotting wood, the dead trees that are already down. Termites are **decomposers**—they feed on and break down the remains of the dead tree so that nutrients in the tree are recycled and turned into soil, and space is made for new living things to grow. Plants need the new soil, and animals need the plants that grow in that soil. So the forest creatures are dependent for their survival on termites and other decomposers, without whom a fallen tree would lie on the forest floor forever.

Where to Find Them

Termites are almost blind because they live in dark, damp spaces inside logs or underground and don't need sight. To find them, look inside rotting logs on the forest floor. Pull off the bark or roll the logs over and look under them; break open logs if you can. (Put the logs and pieces back where you found them when you leave. Other creatures may live there, too.) You can sometimes find termites in the part of a fence post or wooden garden stake that's underground.

When you find one, you usually find a lot because they **forage**, or wander in search of food, in groups. In the damp-wood termite species, the queen lives underground. The termites you see in the log are simply out collecting wood to eat and will soon return to the queen and her young underground. These underground queens are *very* hard to find, but queens of some species live in logs.

Class:	*Insecta*
Order:	*Isoptera (termites only)*
Family:	*Rhinotermitidae (subterranean and damp-wood termites)*
Characteristics:	*Small, soft-bodied, pale-colored, and winged or wingless. Look somewhat like ants but without pinched-in "waist."*
Distribution:	*In all but the very most northern states. More abundant in the Deep South.*
Food:	*Wood or other plant matter.*

How to Catch Them

Termites are very easily injured because their bodies are so soft. You can't just brush them off a log with your fingers into a jar because most will be killed. Use a small paintbrush to sweep them into a jar or onto your hand. They're so tiny they feel tickly on your skin. Let one wander over the back of your arm. They can't jump or run away.

How to Keep Them

Any termites that you catch will probably die soon. They're very sensitive to temperature and the amount of moisture in the air. If it's not just right, they'll die. I've never been able to keep them alive for more than a couple of days. So you may want to consider collecting just a few, or observing them in the woods where you found them.

If you do bring some in, keep them in a jar with a damp, slightly crumpled (not wadded) paper towel with crevices they can crawl into. A cloth lid secured with a rubber band will provide fresh air. You may want to add a little damp crumbly wood.

It's safe to bring a few workers and soldiers into your home, because they can't reproduce. In the most common termite species, workers and soldiers are all that you'll find above ground.

But the queens of some species that are found in the southern and western United States live in logs above ground. For that reason, you don't want to bring a termite-filled log into your home. You also don't want to bring any winged termites inside. They will eventually turn into kings and queens and start new colonies. Please! Not under the tub!

What They Act Like

If you studied a population of ladybugs living in a garden, you'd see that every ladybug has the same job. Each ladybug has to feed itself, protect itself, and mate to make more ladybugs. But termites and their relatives— the ant, bees, and wasps—are **social insects** and live in groups, called **colonies**, with complex social lives. The colony is made up of **castes**, or different body types, which have different jobs in the colony, just as humans do. This **division of labor** is unusual in the animal kingdom.

In any colony of termites, only two, the **king** and **queen**, have the job of making more termites. And that is their only job. They don't feed or protect themselves. Feeding and tending the queen and her eggs and larvae is the job of the **worker** termites. The workers have no children of their own. They feed the queen's children, who are their sisters. They also make repairs on the nest.

The **soldier** termites use their large heads and jaws to protect the whole colony. Occasionally a soldier will bite a human, but it's a weak little bite. You have to admire the soldier's courage. After all, a human could mash it easily. But protecting the colony is the soldier's job, and it will fight to its death to do it.

At certain times of the year the queen lays eggs that grow into winged termites instead of the usual workers and soldiers. The winged termites are destined to become new kings and queens. They fly away and mate, lose their wings, and move underground to start a new colony. The eggs that the new queen lays will grow into workers and soldiers.

If we didn't live in houses with wood frames, we wouldn't think of termites as pests. If we lived in grass or mud huts, we'd think of termites as just another woodland creature—one with a very advanced family system at that. We might even like them in their pudgy whiteness with their brave but puny bite. Lots of animals do like them—as snacks—including toads, centipedes, and our close relatives the chimpanzees. Maybe in another time and place humans munched them, too.

Termites in Board

TENT CATERPILLARS

What They Look Like

When full grown, tent caterpillars are 1 to 2 inches (3 to 5 cm) long, and hairy. Eastern Tent Caterpillars are black with a white stripe on the back. Brown and yellow lines and a row of blue spots run down both sides. Western Tent Caterpillars vary in coloring, but always have a row of white dashes down the back.

Tent caterpillars grow up to be moths with a 1 to 1½-inch (25 to 37 mm) wingspan that are called simply Tent Caterpillar Moths. They're reddish brown to yellow with stout hairy bodies. Each wing has a diagonal white streak on it. But you're much more likely to find the caterpillar than the moth because the tent is so easy to spot. And once you've seen a couple of the caterpillars, they're easy to recognize even without the tent.

When the caterpillars are full size, they spin silken yellowish white cocoons that you might find under outdoor furniture, or on buildings or trees. Inside the cocoon, the caterpillar turns into a moth over a period of about three weeks in summer. The new moths lay eggs which rest all autumn and winter and hatch the next spring. The egg mass looks like a shiny collar around a branch, about ½ inch (12 mm) long.

Tent caterpillars once held up a train! It happened in a small town in New York, where vast numbers of tent caterpillars crawled over the tracks. When the train hit them, its wheels slipped and slid in the mush until it came to a dead stop. The train sat, spinning its wheels, until some slightly green workmen scraped away the slime and sanded the tracks. They say it was two or three days before any of those fellows could eat again!

Tent Caterpillar Moth

Tent Caterpillar

Fortunately, that couldn't happen with just any caterpillar. Most don't occur in a **swarm**—a large number massed together and usually in motion. Tent caterpillars not only slime railroad tracks and roads by getting mashed in great numbers, they can also eat all the leaves off a tree. When I see a bare tree in summer, I often also see the silken tents of the guys that did it. The tents are group homes, nestled in forks of the tree.

Where to Find Them

Eastern Tent Caterpillars make their tents in apple and cherry trees or similar fruit trees. Oak is almost always the home of the western variety. The tent is made in a fork on the branches of the tree and usually doesn't enclose living leaves. (If you find a tent that encloses living leaves and is on the tip of a branch, it's probably the tent of a webworm, a different type of moth.)

One tree can have as many as 50 tents, or only one. The caterpillars usually stay in the silken tent only at night or when it's raining. During the day you might find them anywhere on the tree. May and June are the best months to look.

How to Catch Them

Some caterpillars have spines that sting, so be sure you know what it is before you pick it up. (See the list in the Introduction of other insects not to touch.) If you find a caterpillar in a tent or on a tree with a tent, and

Class:	*Insecta*
Order:	*Lepidoptera (butterflies and moths)*
Family:	*Lasiocampidae (tent caterpillars)*
Genus:	Malacosoma *species*
Characteristics:	*Eastern Tent Caterpillar is hairy and black with a white stripe on the back, and a row of blue spots and brown and yellow lines down each side. Western Tent Caterpillars vary in coloring but always have a row of white dashes down the back.*
Distribution:	*The Eastern Tent Caterpillar is found in all but the West Coast states and parts of the states next to them. The Western Tent Caterpillar is found in western California only.*
Food:	*Eastern Tent Caterpillars eat the leaves of apple and cherry or similar fruit trees. Western Tent Caterpillars eat oak leaves, among others.*

the caterpillar matches the description in this book, you can safely pick it up. Tent caterpillars don't bite or sting. They're soft-bodied and injured easily, so be careful. The adults are attracted to light and you may get one by leaving your porch light on in summer. Catch it against a wall or door with an open jar.

How to Keep Them

Feed your caterpillar leaves of the tree nearest to where you found it. The leaves must be fresh. They'll stay fresh longer if you leave them on the twig and put the end of the twig in water. Three or four caterpillars can be kept comfortably in a quart jar, or as large as necessary to hold a leafy twig and a small glass of water. A cloth lid held on with a rubber band allows air to circulate. Dump out the caterpillars' fras every day so it doesn't pile up in the bottom of the jar. Caterpillars in a dirty jar are more likely to get diseases.

If you supply fresh leaves every day, your caterpillar will probably keep eating and growing. It'll shed its skin several times as it grows. When it gets as big as it's supposed to get, the caterpillar will spin its yellowish white cocoon in a corner of the jar. The cocoon will stay there until the following spring, when a moth will emerge. Either place the cocoon outdoors or let the moth go as soon as it emerges.

What They Act Like

Tent caterpillars are peculiar in several ways. First of all, very few caterpillars build homes. Many can spin a single line of silk to hang from trees, and many can spin silken cocoons to cover themselves when they're ready to turn into moths. But using the silk to make a home is something that puts them on a level with some of our best animal architects, the spiders. Both spiders and caterpillars make silk with their bodies. But while the spinnerets for making silk are on the spider's abdomen, those on the caterpillar are near its mouth.

The tent building is odd, but the fact that the caterpillars do it as a group is even

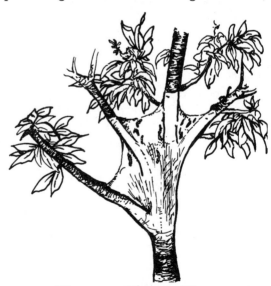

Tent on Cherry Tree

more odd. You won't see a group of spiders making a big community web; instead, each spider makes its own web. The caterpillars get started on their cooperative venture soon after they hatch from the egg. At first the tent is just a single layer wrapped around a fork in the tree. But little caterpillars are poor housekeepers, and the single layer soon fills up with fras, and skins that have been shed. With no mom or dad around to make them clean up, the young ones just add another layer on top, leaving space in between in case someone wants to crawl through. When the second layer gets messy, they add another, and so on until they have a large multilayered tent.

How do tent caterpillars compare with the few other insects that live in groups? The social insects (termites, ants, wasps, and bees) are pros at it. They divide up jobs, communicate complex messages, and take care of each other. Tent caterpillars don't really do much as a group except build the tent. They're a bit below the social level of the bessbugs (described in the next chapter) who not only make a family home, but communicate a little by squeaking, too.

Do aphids qualify as insects that live in a group? Not really. They may be crowded on a plant, but they don't work together or cooperate.

Here's another peculiar thing about tent caterpillars. One scientist discovered that the caterpillars in one tent can have two different "personalities." Some he called "sluggish" and some he called "active." The sluggish caterpillars move very slowly. Sometimes they are so slow they can't even feed themselves! These guys never move very far from the tent. This is bad because it means they might not get enough to eat. It's good because it means they don't mix much with caterpillars from other tents. So they're less likely to pick up illnesses from caterpillars in other groups. Caterpillars can get viruses just as we do, but their viruses are more likely to kill them.

Active larvae crawl all over the tree, much farther away from the tent. They're more likely to get enough food, which is good, but they're also more likely to pick up viruses from members of neighboring tents, which is bad. So each "personality" has an advantage and a disadvantage.

BESSBUGS

What They Look Like

The bessbug is sometimes called the patent-leather beetle because its shiny, smooth black wings and back look like the shoes little girls wear to Sunday School.

It's one of the larger common beetles, about as long as a six-year-old's pinkie finger and almost twice as wide. Each bessbug has a pair of crooked antennae and long jaws that protrude from the front of its head. The larvae are thick, white, wormlike creatures.

This lumbering giant is easy to pick up. Its movements seem to be in slow motion, as if under water. If you do pick it up, it screams! Its thick black legs claw slowly at the air. The shiny black body twists and turns, straining for freedom. Its clumsy jaws open and shut. But it's the scream that really catches your attention—a squeaky little wail. Hey, wait a minute—an insect *squealing*?

Crickets and grasshoppers chirp to attract mates. And lots of insects, like blow flies, make buzzing noises with their wings for no reason. But very few insects make a noise in response to being picked up.

Where to Find Them

A lone bessbug can occasionally be found strolling across a trail or board-walk in a wooded area. But to find several bessbugs, look for rotting logs or stumps where they live. Sometimes you can see signs of bessbugs on the outside of a log—the openings of tunnels on the surface, or little balls of wood fiber on the ground under it. You may find the beetles simply by rolling the log over. If not, you can often pull the top off the rotting log with your hands.

The wood they like is rotten enough to be soft. If you see tunnels inside as wide as a man's thumb, you've probably found bessbugs. A startled beetle in a tunnel may wave its bent antennae at you. "Hey, who turned on the lights?"

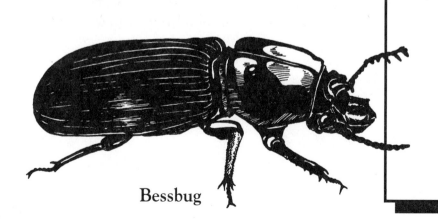

Bessbug

How to Catch Them

Once you've found the beetles, catching them is easy. They don't fly and they're not much faster than a snail. The jaws look a little scary, but a bessbug won't pinch you unless you purposely stick your finger in its mouth. Put the beetles you collect into a jar with a damp paper towel. You'll need to take some of the wood for your buddies to eat.

The larvae will be in the tunnels, too. You might want to leave the larvae and *some* of the adult beetles where they are so the population can recover. Try to leave their home more or less as you found it. Roll the log back where it was and put the top back on it.

How to Keep Them

Keep bessbugs in a plastic dishwashing tub. The wood for them to eat must be well below the top of the tub—4 inches (10 cm) or so—or they'll climb out. They need moisture, so keep the wood damp, but not sodden. Feel the wood every two or three days, and if it feels dry on the bottom, pour a *little* water over it. A damp washcloth over the wood will keep it from drying out so quickly on top.

What They Act Like

Bessbugs are of particular interest because of their social lives. Most insects are solitary as adults. Even if they live in crowded quarters, they don't interact with each other. Aphids, for example, don't feed each other, work cooperatively, or communicate, although there may be hundreds on a plant.

Class:	*Insecta*
Order:	*Coleoptera (beetles)*
Family:	*Passalidae (bessbugs)*
Genus:	Popilius *species*
Characteristics:	*Shiny back, like black patent leather, with parallel grooves running the length of the shiny elytra. Up to 1½ inches (37 mm) in length. Usually found in wood. Make a squeaky sound.*
Distribution:	*Eastern United States and southern Texas.*
Food:	*Damp, rotting wood.*

At the other extreme are the social insects—the termites, ants, wasps, and bees. They live in complicated groups, where jobs are divided among individuals. They communicate complex messages to one another, such as the location of food sources. Sometimes they even give their lives for the benefit of others in the group. For example, worker ants will make a bridge with their bodies, even though they drown, so that other ants in their group may cross a flow of water.

Bessbugs are somewhere between the indifferent aphids and the highly organized ants, termites, bees, and wasps. As the adult beetles eat the wood inside the log, they make tunnels. The tunnels are shared by the adults and all the larvae, who move around freely. So the tunnels are made cooperatively.

They also communicate with each other. Not only do the adults squeak, but the larvae squeak, too! Bessbug larvae squeak for breakfast, which in their case is prechewed wood that mom or dad throws up—yum! The noise of the larva is produced by rubbing the tip of the third leg against the joint of the second leg. An adult beetle makes its squeaks a little differently, by rubbing its elytra against its abdomen. All this squeaking allows the family to keep track of each other in the dark.

So bessbugs feed their young, work together to make tunnels, and communicate within the group. It's true they're not as organized as the social insects—the ants, termites, bees, and wasps. They don't communicate complex messages or give up their lives for the good of the group. But they have a good bit more social interaction than most insects.

I like these guys because they're big enough that they seem scary at first, especially with those big jaws, so holding them makes me feel brave. And I love how they squeak when I pick them up. I think we all love a bug we can talk to.

Bessbug in Container

BUGS THAT COMMUNICATE WITH EACH OTHER IN SPECIAL WAYS

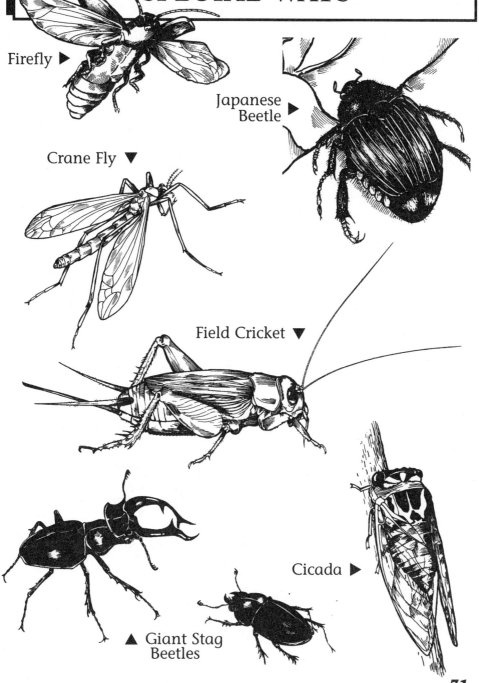

Firefly ▶

Japanese Beetle ▶

Crane Fly ▼

Field Cricket ▼

Cicada ▶

▲ Giant Stag Beetles

FIREFLIES OR _____ LIGHTNING BUGS

What They Look Like

Fireflies, or lightning bugs, are most easily recognized by their glowing abdomens, but they also have a distinctive shape. The adult beetles have a soft shield over the thorax, which covers much of the head as well. Most species are brown or black, with yellow or orange areas. They range in length from ¼ to ¾ inch (6 to 20 mm). The larvae, which resemble mealworms described in a later chapter, also glow. And so do the eggs.

If you see a frog with glowing eardrums or a glowing throat, you'll know it's been eating fireflies. The flickering, magical light of the firefly on summer evenings must catch the frog's attention, just as it does our own. All that blinking seems to be saying, "Catch me!" Why would an insect draw attention to itself in such a way? Why would it make itself so easy to catch? For the same reason birds sing on their perches in spring, or grasshoppers chirp in the grass—to attract mates.

Fireflies aren't the only living things to make their own light. Lots of marine animals do. Along the Outer Banks of North Carolina, I've seen glowing **plankton**, tiny animals or plants that live in water, in the surf at night. Some fungi glow too, such

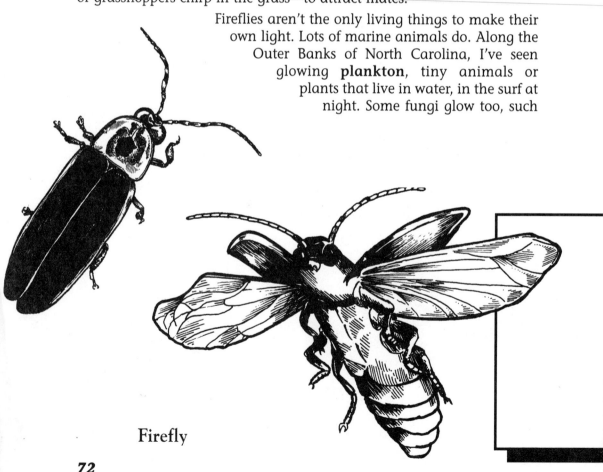

Firefly

as the clusters of orange Jack-o'-lantern mushrooms that you can some-times see in the woods. A few other insects glow. But none of these other creatures are able to turn their lights on and off as fireflies can.

What are fireflies (also called lightning bugs)? They're not really flies *or* true bugs, but beetles of the family Lampyridae. The name comes from the Greek word that is the origin of our word *lamp*.

Where to Find Them

Some fireflies stay in the treetops, some close to the ground, but most fly at just the right height for you to catch them. They fly slowly through the air, flashing at possible mates. One of the most common species prefers lawn areas, while others prefer woods. Spring or early summer evenings just at dark are prime times for finding fireflies.

How to Catch Them

The regular intervals between the firefly's flashes make catching one easy. If you watch a firefly carefully to see where its flashing light moves, you can predict its location at its next flash and be ready to grab it then. You may be tricked, though. Some make a sharp turn after each flash to avoid being caught.

You may be able to attract fireflies to you by using a penlight (a small flashlight). Stand in front of a firefly in flight, wait for exactly two seconds after it flashes, and then give a return flash of ½ second with the penlight. See what happens.

Class:	*Insecta*
Order:	*Coleoptera (beetles)*
Family:	*Lampyridae (fireflies)*
Characteristics:	*Brown or black beetles with yellow or orange markings. Rear segments of abdomen often* **luminous**, *or glowing.*
Distribution:	*Occur throughout the United States except for the northwestern states, north to Manitoba.*
Food:	*Many adult fireflies never eat. Some eat other small creatures.*

How to Keep Them

Keep fireflies in a jar with a damp paper towel and a handful of grass stems for your pets to climb on. Use a cloth lid secured with a rubber band. Try putting the jar of fireflies outdoors for a while in the evening. See if other fireflies are drawn to it. If you keep the jar in your bedroom at night, you'll see their soft glow in the dark.

Adults don't live long and many never eat, even in nature. A few are predators, eating other insects, snails, earthworms—or sometimes other fireflies. Firefly larvae are predators that live on the ground.

Females of some species are wingless and can't fly. They can still flash, though. They're known as glowworms.

What They Act Like

Scientists have spent years working out the details of the signals fireflies use in their flashing. The purpose of the flashing is to attract a mate, but the pattern of blinks is different for each species. A male in flight moves during each flash. He may make a zigzag line, a J shape, a series of dashes, or some other pattern.

The females sit on tall grass stems and watch the show. When a female sees a pattern she recognizes as that of her own species, she flashes back a distinctive, but simpler, message that the male recognizes. Her response may be to wait two seconds, then give a single ½-second flash.

When the male sees her reply, he flies to her and they mate. (The females of a predatory genus called *Photuris* cheat. They copy the flashes of other females and then eat the males they have tricked into flying to them.)

The flash patterns of at least 23 species—male and female—have been worked out. Wouldn't it be fun to discover another pattern? With your penlight, you could be the first to communicate with that species.

How do fireflies make their glow? And how do they turn it on and off? Scientists have been studying the firefly

Firefly Flashing
(male)

glow for over 100 years. Some scientists have used so many fireflies in their research that they've had to buy fireflies from children or anyone else willing to collect the insects for them. Because of all this studying, we know now that the firefly's glow is produced by a series of chemical reactions involving two substances inside the firefly's abdomen. The first of these substances, **luciferin**, is a pigment that produces light (but no heat) when it undergoes a chemical change called oxidation. The second substance, **luciferase**, is an enzyme (a type of protein) that causes luciferin to undergo a chemical change and give off light.

The light given off may be a true yellow, or it may have a blue, red, or green tint, depending on the species of firefly. Even after a firefly dies, the belly will keep on glowing for a while. The firefly's light, or any other light produced by a living thing, is called **bioluminescence**.

In some of the most recent firefly research, scientists have learned how to transfer the glowing ability of fireflies to tobacco plants. (No one needs glowing tobacco—the scientists just wanted to see if they could do it.) In other new research, doctors have learned how to use luciferin and luciferase to make a light that helps them find damaged cells in people. Fireflies are not only interesting but helpful.

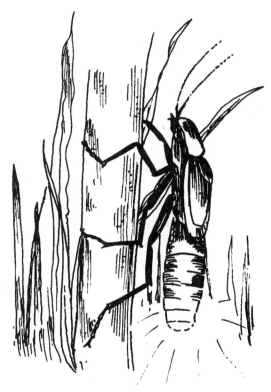

Firefly Flashing
(female)

CRANE FLIES

What They Look Like

Crane flies look very much like huge, very clumsy mosquitoes. Their stilt-like legs are so long that some species, with legs stretched out, could fill a small saucer! In addition to the long spindly legs, they have long slender bodies and long narrow wings as well. Their wings stick out widely from the body when at rest. "Slim" might be a good name for a pet crane fly.

Anyone who mistakes a crane fly for a giant mosquito might be a little nervous about the long spike on the end of the female's body. A giant stinger? No, just an **ovipositor**, or egg-depositor, that she uses to get her eggs underground. Crane flies don't sting and they don't even bite, unlike their cousins, the blood-sucking mosquitoes. Crane flies have no piercing mouthparts. Some adults live such short lives, they never eat at all. Others eat flower nectar.

Like mosquitoes, crane flies are brownish or gray. Crane flies and mosquitoes are both types of flies, in the order Diptera. Their larvae, though, are very different. A few crane fly species have larvae that live in water as mosquito larvae

Crane Fly Larva

do, but most live in the soil. One famous type of crane fly larva is a tough gray character, called a leatherjacket because of its leathery skin. Leatherjackets can ruin a lawn by eating the grass roots. But the larvae of most species eat only dead plants and are harmless.

The spindly adults are not good fliers. They fly awkwardly, with the second and third pair of legs dragging behind.

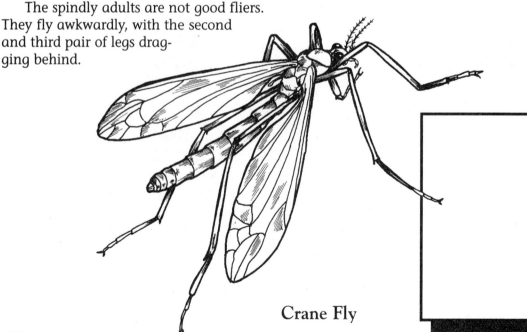

Crane Fly

Where to Find Them

Crane flies can be found most often indoors at night. The adults are attracted to light. They bumble and bounce across the wall as if drunk, their four back legs hanging below. Crane flies tend to be found in moist, damp areas with a lot of vegetation. In autumn they sometimes gather in swarms and dance a few feet above the ground or water. They may bob up and down and land on the water like water striders.

How to Catch Them

You can catch a crane fly with a jar. Just pop the jar over it and stick a piece of cardboard under the jar. Although they're big, they're easy to catch because they're such poor fliers and so clumsy. They're not only easy for you to catch, but also for birds and flying insect predators, like robber flies, who swoop down on them like a duck on a junebug. They haven't a chance.

To hold one, dump it from the jar onto your palm. It will stand there willingly, if your hand is big enough for all the legs to get a footing. Then it will take off to bumble against the wall some more.

How to Keep Them

Crane flies may be kept alive in captivity for a few days with a damp paper towel for moisture. A jar is too small for the long legs. A terrarium, 10 × 20 inches (25 × 50 cm), will allow room for flying, but a smaller one will do. Crane flies won't squeeze through cracks, so a newspaper laid across the top of your terrarium will do for a lid.

Keep more than one at a time if you like. They won't bother each other and may court and mate if you're lucky. You can offer fresh flowers since some are said to eat flower nectar. But pet crane flies probably won't eat. At any rate, the adults live very short lives—a matter of days.

Class:	*Insecta*
Order:	*Diptera (flies)*
Family:	*Tipulidae (crane flies)*
Characteristics:	*Very much like giant mosquitoes, with very long legs.*
Distribution:	*Throughout the United States.*
Food:	*Many adults never eat; some eat flower nectar.*

What They Act Like

You might wonder why crane flies have such very long and gangly legs. What use are they? One use for them was worked out in some very clever experiments by a scientist named Stich. Stich discovered that males and females recognize each other as future mates only when they happen to accidentally bump legs. They can fly all around each other, but nothing will happen unless the legs touch. This touch triggers inside them the beginning of the courtship process.

Stich proved this by showing that males will respond just as well to fake legs made of wire or thread. When a male is bumped by a leg, real or fake, he grabs it and waits for the female crane fly to raise one of her other legs. Her leg-raising is a signal to the male that means, "Okay, I'm willing." If her signal gives him the go-ahead, he proceeds with courtship (including "kissing" the back of her head), and then mating.

It would be easy to try to repeat Stich's experiment. You may be able to figure out whether a pet crane fly is a male or female. Make a fake leg with some very thin wire, or use a small thread from some twine that has been unraveled. You can stiffen a piece of sewing thread by putting a little laundry starch on it and letting it dry. Better yet, find a dead crane fly or daddy-long-legs and use one of its legs.

Put your hand in the terrarium and touch the leg of your crane fly with the fake leg. How does it react? If it responds by raising one of its legs, that means it's a female who thinks you're a male! If your crane fly moves away or doesn't react when you touch its leg, it may mean you have a male. Or you may have a female who is not fooled by your fake leg.

How do you think a crane fly would react to a daddy-long-legs? Their legs are very similar. Put the two together in a terrarium and see if the daddy-long-legs happens to bump legs with the crane fly accidentally. How does your crane fly react? Can it be fooled into responding to the wrong animal? Daddy-long-legs sometimes eat other insects, but your crane fly may see this strange visitor as a sweetheart rather than a potential predator.

Crane Flies Bumping Legs

STAG BEETLES

What They Look Like

Stag beetles are solid, heavy beetles, brown or reddish-brown or black. The broad flat head and awesome jaws are the features that make an easy identification—the head of a deer on the body of a beetle! Well, almost. The *antlers* of a deer anyway, with branching points just like the real thing. Male deer are called stags, and the family of fearsome stag beetles are named for them.

Only the males have the huge antlers, which are really jaws, so it's easy to tell male and female apart. The female is just a plain beetle, with normal-looking beetle jaws. She may be big, up to 1½ inches (38 mm) long, but not as big as the male. One species, the Giant Stag Beetle, can reach 2½ to 3 inches (63 to 75 mm) in length, and the jaws take up a third of that length. The head of the Giant Stag Beetle is almost ¾ inch (2 cm) wide, to hold up the 1-inch (25 mm) long jaws. The larvae look like small, fat, white worms.

Class:
Insecta

Order:
Coleoptera (beetles)

Family:
Lucanidae (stag beetles)

Characteristics:
Males are up to 2½ inches (63 mm) long, with large jaws that resemble the antlers of a deer.

Distribution:
Stag beetles are distributed throughout the eastern United States and adjacent regions of Canada; also California to British Columbia. The Giant Stag Beetle (Lucanus elaphus) occurs in the states east of Oklahoma, north to Illinois.

Food:
Sap oozing from live trees.

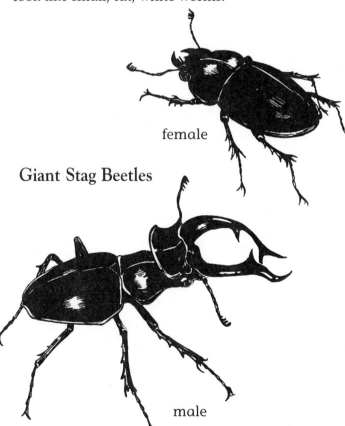

female

Giant Stag Beetles

male

Bessbugs are another type of large beetle found around logs, as stag beetles are. You can tell them from female stag beetles by the very shiny exoskeleton or outer covering of the bessbug that looks like black patent leather. Also the bessbugs have lots of very distinct parallel grooves running down the length of their elytra.

Where to Find Them

Try looking in a wooded area around rotting stumps and logs, and on the ground. Stag beetles are one of those creatures that are hard to find at a moment's notice. Like mantises and walkingsticks, they turn up in their own sweet time. You may see six or seven in one summer, or none at all.

How to Catch Them

Adults are attracted to light, so you may catch one by leaving porch lights on at night, especially if you live near woods. The beetles may stay on the ground near the light even after dawn.

If you come upon one, the jaws can be a little scary. Often the stag beetle will rear back, with his head up and jaws open, when it is disturbed. The jaws are actually very weak, though the female can pinch you. You can avoid the jaws by picking the beetle up from the back.

How to Keep Them

Stag beetles do fine as temporary pets, but not for a long time. They eat sap that oozes from live trees, which is not easy to provide indoors. You can give them a comfortable resting place for a few days in a terrarium with soil or sand or a log, and a damp paper towel for moisture.

What They Act Like

When stag beetles court, the two huge males face each other across the log, ready for another clash, as the female watches silently nearby. She knows the winner of the combat will be her mate. Suddenly one male charges again, his "antlers" or jaws crashing into those of the other. They push against one another, struggling. One flips over, then slips off the log and is gone.

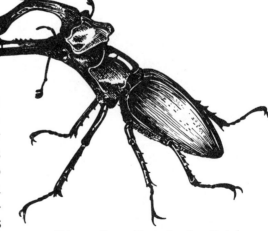

Giant Stag Beetle (male)

Dead? No, these fierce fighters can't hurt each other, for all their jaw clacking. The jaws are too big to be powerful. Imagine holding a pair of foot-long tongs at the hinge and trying to pinch your brother or sister. You couldn't get much power into the pinch. Now imagine a pair of nail-clipping scissors. Plenty of force there. The female has short jaws, like the scissors, and can deliver a good pinch.

After a male has won a battle with another male, he and the female mate, and then she lays her eggs on or around rotting logs or stumps. The eggs hatch into larvae that eat the rotting wood, making their way through it as they grow, with strong jaws like their mothers'. When they're big enough, they become pupae, and then emerge as adult beetles.

These guys really know how to attract attention. One turned up at a gas station, and the attendant carried him around on a rag, showing him to all the customers in amazement. He was hoping someone could identify the terrible creature, or maybe he was just sharing his surprise.

Stag beetles may be the most startling insect you'll ever see. Finding one will make you gape. It's not the kind of creature you can glance at and pass on by. Like the gas station attendant, you'll feel compelled to find someone to look with you—someone else to startle. What an awesome display of weapons, even if they are mostly for show.

FIELD CRICKETS

What They Look Like

Field crickets are homely little creatures—plain brown or black, with knobby knees like grasshoppers' sticking up above their backs. They also have two little feelers on the back ends of their bodies called cerci. The cerci tell them if someone is sneaking up behind them. Tickle your cricket's cerci and see what it does!

In between the cerci a female has a long ovipositor that she rams down into the sand to lay her eggs. If she sticks the ovipositor in between the sand and the glass of a terrarium, you can sometimes see the eggs coming out, one at a time. Egg laying is a favorite pastime of the females'.

You'd never guess to look at field crickets that they're wrestlers. They scuttle about, looking for dark places to hide, as though they were as wimpy as roaches. Their knobby legs look innocent enough, but they're used as weapons. If you were another cricket, you might be kicked in the face several times a day! In fact, a cricket will sometimes kick your finger if you tickle his cerci.

Where to Find Them

Field crickets are one of the easiest animals to find. They hide under dead plants, rocks, garbage cans, and leaf piles. You can find them under piles of grass clippings, too; get out the rake and drag it through the dying lawn a few times. The most crickets I've ever seen in one place outside were under a heavy trash bag left on a patch of gravel for three weeks.

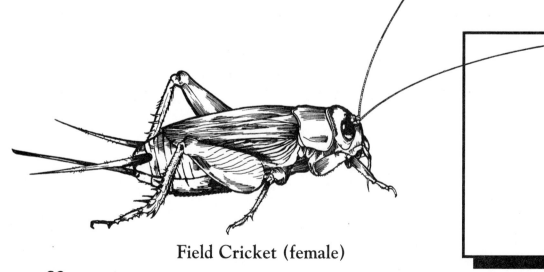

Field Cricket (female)

How to Catch Them

Catching crickets can be a lot of fun if you're in the mood. It's something you learn to be good at. Here's the trick: use a jar. Take two jars—one for catching, and the other for holding them. Slowly flip over the leaves on top of a leaf pile until you get down to the damp part. When the crickets come out, they stand there just for a moment, as if trying to get used to the light. You have to slap the jar down hard and fast, so the rim of the jar presses down into the leaves. Then you wiggle your hand under the jar and you've got one.

If your neighborhood friends wander up, they'll try to grab the crickets with their hands, but they'll probably fail. The crickets just wiggle away too easily from a hand. But where the crickets have no leaves or grass to wiggle into, such as on the bare ground under a garbage can, you'll have better luck catching them with just your hands.

How to Keep Them

Keep crickets in a terrarium with about 1 inch (25 mm) of damp sand in the bottom. The females need the damp sand for egg laying. Put water for them in the lid of either a film can or a small jar. Crickets love tunnels, so throw in a toilet paper tube or make

Field Cricket in Toilet Paper Tube

Class:	*Insecta*
Order:	*Orthoptera (orthopterans)*
Family:	*Gryllidae (crickets)*
Genus:	Gryllus *species*
Characteristics:	*Dark brown insects, up to 1 inch (25 mm) long, with wings and long, grasshopperlike back legs. (The "knees" of the back legs stick up above the back.) Found under things on the ground.*
Distribution:	*Throughout North America to Alaska.*
Food:	*Decaying vegetation and sometimes meat.*

some tunnels in the sand with a pencil.

Crickets will eat about any kind of fruit or vegetable or bread. They'll even eat meat—each other! If a cricket dies in the container, the others will munch him for some extra protein. They'll eat their nymphs too, when they first hatch from the eggs, so you have to remove the adults if you want your hatchlings to grow up.

I usually feed my crickets a piece of raw apple every day. You could also give them a few Cheerios™ or a piece of dry dog food that has been soaked in water.

What They Act Like

Field crickets will chirp, chirp, chirp. Sometimes it can get on your nerves. If I'm trying to work, I may have to put them in another room and shut the door. Why are they always chirping? It's always the males; the females don't make any noise. And a male by himself won't do it because he has no one to chirp to. They make the sound by rubbing one wing against another.

A loud chirp is a male-to-male chirp. It means, "Get out of here!" Crickets usually live far apart in nature and they like it that way. Each has his own little space. Just as a dog will bark when you go in his yard, a cricket will chirp if another cricket comes into his space.

And it doesn't stop at chirping. If you put a male cricket in a terrarium with a film can on its side for a little house, he'll get to thinking he's got it made—a little house all his own. If you put a female in there with him, then he's really on cloud nine. (You can tell a female by the long ovipositor described earlier.) After a day or so get another male and mark him with a dot of white paint just behind his head (so you can tell them apart). Put the second male in the terrarium. Now you'll see some action, but you have to watch carefully.

The first cricket, the homeowner, will stalk and corner the new male, chirping loudly at him now and then. He may raise his head end or back end, which in cricket language is like shaking your fist in someone's face. If the new cricket gets behind the homeowner, he can expect a swift kick in the face. The kicks are fast; you have to watch carefully.

As the crickets get madder, they may butt heads. But the grand finale, which I've seen only a couple of times, is wrestling. Here the homeowner hops on the newcomer and rolls him over and over on the sand! It's a wonderful sight. They don't hurt each other, since they have no stinger or strong jaws. Leave them together to work out a truce, or separate them for a future encounter on another day.

The male-to-female chirp sounds different. If a male chirps to a female, he's trying to get her to be his mate. He chirps very softly, rocking gently back and forth while clawing gently at the sand. He looks so desperate for her attention, you kind of feel sorry for him—especially when you see how she reacts. She often backs up to him and kicks him in the face! But he keeps at it. Even if he finds a female to mate with him, the next day he's desperately searching again.

Crickets have busy social lives for such homely little things. If they're not tunneling, they're picking a fight or trying to find a sweetheart—always on the go. It's nice for us that they carry on their little dramas out in the open where we can watch. For entertainment, field crickets rank right there at the top.

CICADAS

What They Look Like

The body of the adult cicada similar to the body of the nymph in shape—1 inch (25 mm) long, and thick and chunky. The adults of most cicada species are blackish, often with greenish markings. The head is wide, with large bulging eyes. The adult's wings are transparent and extend well behind the body. Some people confuse cicadas with locusts, a type of grasshopper. Locusts and other grasshoppers have big back legs for jumping, and their "knees" stick way up above their backs. Cicadas have short back legs.

You've probably seen "cicada skins" clinging to trees. They're about 1 inch (25 mm) long, a light clear brown, and brittle. You can tell they're empty by looking through the slit on the back of the skin. What you've found is just the outer covering, or **exoskeleton**, that the animal left behind. The front legs of the exoskeleton have sharp down-pointing hooks that hold it to a tree (or your shirt or hair).

The exoskeleton belongs to the nymph, who starts out no bigger than an ant and spends its life underground, eating and growing very slowly. Nymphs of some species stay underground for 17 years! When a nymph is finally old enough to metamorphose (change) into an adult, it crawls out of its hole in the ground and up the nearest tree. There it clings with its heavy front legs, while its exoskeleton splits down the back. A brand new adult crawls out, leaving the exoskeleton for you to find.

Adult
emerging
from
exoskeleton

Empty
exoskeleton
of cicada
nymph

**Cicada Shedding
Exoskeleton**

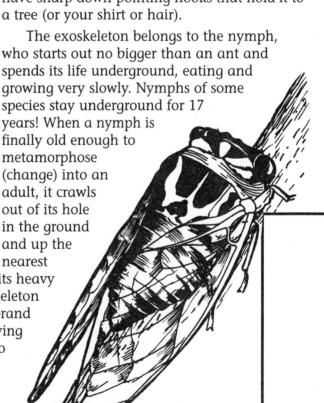

Adult Cicada

If you hang exoskeletons around in different places, some people will think they're alive. And if you like to startle people, an exoskeleton hanging on your shirt or in your hair is a good way to do it. People will ask, "What is that brown beetle-thing in your hair?"

Where to Find Them

In July and August cicadas can be heard buzzing loudly in the trees, but getting them down is another matter. If you look on the ground under a tree when you hear them buzzing, you may find cicada holes in the dirt, ½ to 1 inch (12 to 25 mm) across. They're so deep you can't see the bottom, and so they look black. On rare occasions, you may find a young cicada, or nymph, in one of the holes, just below the opening, like a worm peeking out of its hole. If a nymph is at the hole's opening, it's getting ready to come out, to crawl up a tree and shed its exoskeleton.

The adult cicadas begin to die in August and September. As they grow weaker, they can be found on sidewalks and on the ground under trees, too weak to fly. The healthy ones stay in the treetops, buzzing loudly.

The sound is so loud it seems to be coming from everywhere, much louder than any other insect noise. Sometimes the sound is steady, sometimes it pulsates. *Screee-uh-screee-uh-screee*...nonstop. Some cicada species can be heard over ½ mile (0.8 km) away! Grasshopper or cricket noises are more likely to come from grass, or other plants close to the ground. Frog calls are usually near water. Cicada calls come from trees and fill the air.

Class:	*Insecta*
Order:	*Homoptera (homopterans)*
Family:	*Cicadidae (cicadas)*
Characteristics:	*Thick and blackish with green markings, long transparent wings, and widely spaced bulging eyes.*
Distribution:	*Throughout the United States except the Northwest.*
Food:	*Plant juices.*

How to Catch Them

A nymph getting ready to emerge from its hole can sometimes be pulled out gently. Their front legs are very strong, for digging and climbing trees, or hanging on. You may find it more fun to leave the nymph in its hole and watch it over the next few hours as it leaves the hole and climbs a tree. You may get to see its exoskeleton split and a new adult emerge, leaving the exoskeleton on the tree.

If you happen to come upon a new adult just emerging from its exoskeleton, watch without touching. Before it can fly, it must pump blood into the veins of the wings so they will unfurl and straighten out. Within a few hours the wings will be dry and hardened and ready for flight. If you disturb the cicada, its wings may be damaged permanently. This is a dangerous time for cicadas—birds eat a lot of them before their wings harden.

Since adult cicadas found on the ground are usually weak, they don't resist being picked up. (A healthy one will just fly away.) You can lift it by grasping it gently between two fingers. Put it on your arm, the back of your hand, or your shirt front. Claws at the ends of their legs allow the cicadas to cling to anything. Several times I've had adult cicadas cling to my arm or shirt for hours, barely moving, as I've gone about my business at work. People say, "What is that? How do you get it to stay there?" They think I've trained it; they don't know it's just weak.

Sometimes an adult cicada will slowly swing down its strawlike mouthpart and try to suck plant sap from my hand. I've never been punctured, but if this possibility makes you uncomfortable, put it on your shirt instead of your skin. Those too weak to fly are usually too weak to try to eat, too. They have no jaws or stinger and so can't bite or sting.

If it has enough strength, a cicada may buzz in your hand, especially if you hold it between two fingers. I think the buzzing is an attempt to startle you into letting it go. If you put it on the floor, it may zip around on its back, unable to stand or fly. Or a stronger one may fly to the ceiling, where an older person can easily recapture the cicada for you by standing on a chair.

How to Keep Them

Adults may be kept indoors with a damp sponge or paper towel for moisture. They probably won't live more than a day or two, whether you keep them or let them go. Most that are weak enough to be captured are too weak to escape, so a jar and lid are probably unnecessary. You can offer them leaves or twigs of the tree closest to where you found them, or closest to the buzzing sound, but I've never observed an adult eating in captivity.

What They Act Like

We humans spend most of our lives as adults. But lots of insects, such as the cicadas, do it backward. Cicadas spend up to 17 years as nymphs, or youngsters, and only about six weeks as adults. This arrangement is actually pretty common in the insect world, although the cicada is an extreme example. Some adult moths live such a short period that they don't even have mouths! You may remember that adults of some lacewing species never eat. Their adult lives are over in a few days.

Adult insects have only one mission in life—to mate and have babies. For a female, mating means finding a male to fertilize her eggs so they'll start to grow. Mating and laying eggs doesn't take very long, so there is no need for adult insects to linger on.

For mammals (including humans), adult life is not so simple. Mammals not only mate and have babies, but also take care of them until the babies are grown, which can take a number of years. Mammals may also help take care of grandchildren. Insects almost never take care of their young. (The bessbugs and social insects are exceptions.) Egg laying is the end of most insects' parental duties, and the end of their adult duties.

Female cicadas can damage trees with their egg laying. They make slits or holes in twigs for their eggs, usually so many slits that the twigs fall off the trees. The eggs hatch into ant-size nymphs, which fall to the ground and right away use their strong front legs to burrow into the ground—some go more than a foot deep. And there they stay—some for two or three years, some for much longer.

The job of young, immature insects is always to eat and grow until they are big enough to become adults. But why should the nymph, or immature cicada, take *so* long to grow up? Cicada nymphs feed on tree roots. They feed on a type of fluid in the tree root that's very watery and low in nutrients, so their growing is very slow.

You're more likely to notice the noisy buzzing of cicadas than anything else about them. Grasshoppers and crickets make a similar sort of sound, although quieter, by rubbing one body part against another—often one wing against another. But cicadas don't do any rubbing. A cicada has a very tight **membrane**, a thin layer of skin on its body, that makes a noise in the same way a metal box makes a noise when you pop the lid in and out. A tight muscle attached to the membrane pulls it inward so that it buckles with a click. When the muscle relaxes, the membrane—the "lid"—pops back out. A big air sac inside the cicada's body makes the sound louder, just as the hollow body of a drum makes the vibration of a drumhead louder.

The membrane on the cicada is popped in and out so quickly that the sounds run together and sound like a buzz. Only the male cicadas produce a noise. Like most calling animals, they do it to attract mates.

JAPANESE BEETLES

What They Look Like

The beautiful Japanese Beetle is about ½ inch (12 mm) long. It's a deep shiny green, with coppery or brownish-orange wing covers, or elytra, that don't quite reach to the end of its back. The claws on its back legs enable it to hold on easily to almost anything.

Japanese Beetles are in a family of insects called scarab beetles. Scarab beetles are often a brilliant metallic blue or green, or more than one color, like scarab bracelets that have several colored stones, or scarabs, linked together in a chain. They're wide, thick beetles, very rounded across the back, and their antennae are different from those of all other beetles. Their antennae have on the end a roundish club that can spread apart like four or five pages of a book or squeezed lightly together to make a little ball. Often the males have horns. The Rhinoceros Beetle is one species of scarab beetle that has a horn, which looks just like a miniature rhinoceros horn.

Adult Japanese Beetles eat leaves and fruits, and they sometimes eat in huge groups—100 beetles on one peach! The larvae, called grubs, eat roots and can eat all the roots of a lawn, so you can roll the grass back like a carpet!

Japanese Beetles look a lot like the Green June Beetle, whose wings and body both are deep green. The wings are velvety green, the body a shiny green. The Green June Beetle is a bit bigger than the Japanese Beetle, at ¾ inch (2 cm), and doesn't feed in such huge groups. It's not really considered a pest, although its diet is similar to that of its Japanese cousin.

Japanese Beetle

Where to Find Them

Japanese Beetles like roses a lot, and other flowering plants that home-owners put in their yards, like zinnias and hollyhocks. Look for them in gardens or on shrubs, especially flowering shrubs, or fruit trees in your neighborhood, such as peach, apple, and cherry trees. You might find them on elm, birch, linden, and lots of other trees. Ask your neighbors if they've seen any Japanese Beetles.

Because Japanese Beetles are pests, you may be able to locate a horde of them by calling a hardware store or the county extension service, which your parents can help you find in the phone book. Traps and bait for Japanese Beetles are sold at hardware stores. The beetles are attracted by the smells of flowers and the bait has a similar smell, at least to the beetles. The folks that work at the hardware store often talk to their customers—gardeners and farmers—so they're likely to know where problem areas are. And they can sell you the traps and bait to catch the beetles.

Japanese Beetles Eating Rose

Class:	*Insecta*
Order:	*Coleoptera*
Family:	*Scarabaeidae (scarab beetles)*
Genus and species:	Popillia japonica
Characteristics:	*A deep, shiny green beetle with coppery or brownish-orange elytra.*
Distribution:	*Most common in the eastern United States, often in huge clusters.*
Food:	*Leaves, flowers, and fruit of many different plants.*

How to Catch Them

Japanese Beetles fly, but they're not so fast that you can't grab them. They don't bite, although the hooks on their legs feel prickly. You may want to try a trap—a four-sided plastic box, with lots of openings, that hangs from a tree. This box has hooks on the bottom to hold a bag. The special bait goes in the box to attract the beetles. When they fly to the bait, they slip on the smooth surface of the box and fall into the bag. They can't get out and will eventually die from lack of food and water, unless you take them out. Because Japanese Beetles are considered pests, you'll need to keep any that you remove for observation until they die a natural death.

If you get a trap, put it in an area where beetles have already been seen. Your parents and neighbors probably won't want you to attract the beetles to their yards. The best place is a field or other area where no one lives and where there are no special plants that someone cares about.

How to Keep Them

Transfer some of the beetles from your trap to a jar or terrarium. A cloth lid held in place with a rubber band provides ventilation. Offer your pets a piece of fruit, such as peach or apple, or *fresh* leaves. Try lots of different kinds, and see how many they'll accept. If the fruit is juicy, they need no other moisture. Otherwise, a damp paper towel can provide water.

What They Act Like

All insects that are not social insects have to be able to find others when it's time to mate. How do they do it? Different ones use different senses. Crickets and cicadas use hearing. Their loud noises are made by males, calling females to come join them.

Another sense animals use to communicate with each other is sight. Fireflies use their eyes to pick up messages—the blinking patterns of males and the simple response flash of the female. Japanese Beetles use another sense to find a partner for mating. It's not hearing or sight, nor is it touch or taste. It's smell. And this time it's the female and not the male who starts the communicating.

A scent produced by an animal that causes another individual of the same species to respond in a particular way is called a **pheromone**. The pheromone produced by the female Japanese Beetle is a very powerful perfume that the male can't resist. When the male Japanese Beetle smells it, he follows the scent through the air until he finds the female, which is in itself quite a feat. Some Japanese Beetle traps are baited with the female smell, and males can find it from as far as 500 feet (152 m)—the length of more than one and a half football fields! Can you imagine finding a beetle from that distance simply by *smelling* it? It's pretty amazing what the "lowly" critters can do! They say humans produce pheromones, too, that affect our reactions to each other without our really knowing it.

The Japanese Beetle is so much more of a problem than other scarab species because it is an **introduced species**—a species that has been brought to one region of the world from another. The Green June Beetle, on the other hand, is a **native species**—a species that lives naturally in the area in which it first appeared. The Japanese Beetle was brought from Japan to this country by accident in 1916, in the roots of a plant. It has since spread out and made quite a pest of itself. Kudzu, an introduced plant that was brought here from Japan, is also a pest. It grows over native plants and sometimes kills them. The starling is an introduced bird that was brought here from Europe. Its numbers have grown so much that it has become a pest, taking over most of the spots that bluebirds might have used for nesting and leaving the bluebirds with no homes. Starlings also compete with native birds for food.

Introduced species multiply so fast because they've been here such a short time that they have no natural enemies to limit their numbers. It can take millions of years for a species to **evolve**, or undergo the changes that adapt it more closely to its changing environment. No native species has had time to evolve a special ability to find and eat these introduced species. In Japan, or the other foreign countries introduced species come from, they have natural enemies because they've been there millions of years. Animals around them have had plenty of time to evolve the ability to eat them.

When left alone, nature provides her own balances in this way. If a food source exists, something will evolve along with it to take advantage of it. So in nature, no population grows out of control. When humans step in, they more often than not cause far-reaching disturbances. One thing we can do to control these imported pests is to import some of their natural enemies. And scientists are working on that—but very carefully. Sometimes the remedy can cause other problems we didn't predict. Nature works best when left alone.

BUGS THAT MULTIPLY— BEFORE YOUR EYES!

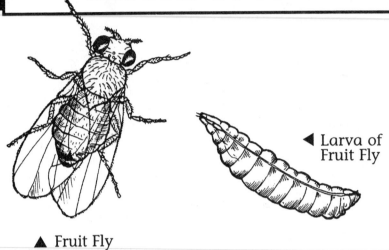

◀ Larva of Fruit Fly

▲ Fruit Fly

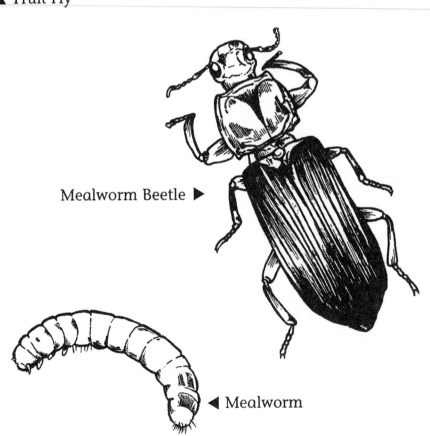

Mealworm Beetle ▶

◀ Mealworm

MEALWORMS

What They Look Like

Mealworms, the larvae of mealworm beetles, are white, slim, and worm-like, and about 1 inch (25 mm) long. Mealworms beetles are rather narrow, dark brown or black, and about half as long as mealworms. They are slow-moving, awkward, and do not fly.

The mealworm does not make a cocoon in its pupal stage the way many insects do. Moth caterpillars spin a cocoon around themselves as they change. Butterflies hide inside a chrysalis. Fly pupae (maggots) are covered in little, smooth, cigarlike cases as they metamorphose. But on a mealworm pupa you can see the outline of legs and head and eyes. They seem tightly wrapped against the body, or not quite formed.

The metamorphosis of the mealworm is a little like the famous story of Dr. Jekyll and Mr. Hyde. Dr. Jekyll is a regular kind of guy, a scientist who mixes a secret drink in his laboratory that turns him into the evil and hideous Mr. Hyde. As the drink wears off, he turns slowly back to the mild-mannered Dr. Jekyll. The meek little mealworm—Dr. Jekyll—looks sort of like a small white caterpillar, harmless and not remarkable in any way. But when the mealworm is about as long as your little toe (but much

Class:
Insecta
Order:
Coleoptera (beetles)
Family:
Tenebrionidae (darkling beetles)
Genus:
Tenebrio *species (mealworm beetles)*
Characteristics:
A plain, dark brown or black beetle about ½ inch (12 mm) long. Moves slowly and awkwardly. Larvae are slim and wormlike, about 1 inch (25 mm) long.
Distribution:
In pet stores everywhere; sometimes in fish bait stores.
Food:
Grain or grain products. In captivity, oat bran or wheat bran.

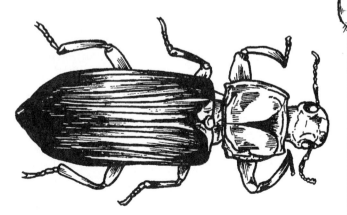

Mealworm

Mealworm Beetle

thinner), it wiggles out of its skin one day and what's underneath is—Mr. Hyde! The mealworm pupa is one of the oddest-looking creatures you'll ever see. It looks like an alien from outer space, or a mummy! This Mr. Hyde-ish creature is very different from the plain little mealworm. If you found one and didn't know what it was, you might think it was just some dead weird thing. But then, it twitches! *Did* it twitch or did you imagine it? It did! Hey—what kind of weird shrunken thing is this that can't do anything but *twitch?*

After about two weeks, something wiggles from the pupa's skin. Out comes a beautifully delicate, brand new beetle, soft and white, but hardening quickly and turning dark brown. You've witnessed one of the miracles of nature! Dr. Jekyll to Mr. Hyde and back to ordinary—this time a beetle.

Where to Find Them/How to Catch Them

Mealworms live under the bark of dead trees—but so do lots of other beetles. There are about 300,000 different types of beetles in the world! And mealworm beetles are not very distinctive looking, so it would be hard to tell if a beetle you found under the bark of a tree was a mealworm beetle or not, unless you'd seen them before. A much easier way to get mealworms is to buy them at a pet store. They're sold as food for lizards. (Toads like them, too.) They're also sold as fish bait at some places that carry fishing supplies. Look in the yellow pages of your phone book under "Fisherman's Supplies" or "Pet Supplies."

How to Keep Them

All you need to keep mealworms is a plastic dishwashing tub and a box of wheat bran or oat bran from the cereal section of a grocery store. Pour the whole box, dry and uncooked, into the dishwashing tub. The bran should be 1 to 3 inches (25 to 76 mm) deep. If you want your mealworms to grow up and make more mealworms, you need to start with at least 10 or 20 individuals. The bran will last a long time, several weeks or maybe months.

You don't have to provide any water for them, but they seem to do better if you add a raw potato slice every week or so. They suck moisture from the potato. The mealworms also seem to do better if you keep a paper towel over the bran. You can moisten the paper towel a little, twice a week or so, instead of adding a potato slice. The paper towel will make them stay on the surface of the bran, where they are more visible.

The mealworms shed their skins several times as they grow, so you'll see the skins in the bran. You'll also see the bodies of adult beetles that have died. The bodies will simply dry out; they don't need to be removed.

What They Act Like

An individual mealworm doesn't get much reaction out of anyone—just a dry, plain, little wormlike thing. But get a bunch of mealworms together, get them wiggling, and now you've got something that'll make almost anyone murmur, "Oh, gross." A handful of twisting and turning mealworms probably reminds people of maggots, which are really fly larvae. Maggots are very different though. Maggots often live in and eat foul rotting material, like rotting meat, garbage, or dog droppings. This stuff has lots of bacteria, or germs, in it, so maggots are not clean. They also have wet skins and look slimy, which does not add to their appeal. But mealworms are perfectly clean. Bran is not full of germs and has no odor, and both bran and mealworms are dry. It's just the *cluster* of wiggling mealworms that gets people thinking about maggots.

If you do want to get an "Oh, how disgusting!" reaction from someone, put into your mealworm tub a small, *slightly* damp piece of sponge or foam rubber the size of a Ping-Pong ball. The next day it will look like the head of Medusa, a person in a Greek myth who had snakes for hair! The mealworms' mouths will be on the sponge, while their wiggling, squirming back ends are free.

Without a damp sponge or a paper towel to peek under, you won't see a lot of action in a mealworm tub. Three or four mealworm beetles may lie sluggishly on the surface of the bran, while a couple of beetles tool around. But put your ear down close to the bran and you'll *hear* the action. You can hear a rustling sound—the munching and wiggling of dozens of little mouths and bodies.

The adult beetles are less likely to get any reaction. What bland little bugs! The beetles, like the mealworms, are easy insects to pick up and

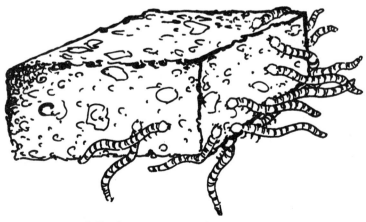

Mealworms on Sponge

hold. Not only are they harmless, but sometimes helpless, too. Turn a beetle on its back and see. They have an awful time righting themselves, and seem to get in this pitiful position much too often.

Both mealworms and beetles have definite ideas about where they like to hang out. Try offering them a choice in a terrarium between a damp paper towel or a dry paper towel, both flat. Or offer a choice between a brightly lit and a shaded area. Give them at least an hour to make a decision.

Both beetles and mealworms are solid and hardy critters. They can get by with a lot of neglect from their human keepers. And these innocent and humble servants to humankind, with no means of escape or defense, often wind up as dinner for some pet. Maybe a greater contribution to us is the bug's-eye view of metamorphosis—mealworm to pupa to adult—before our very eyes.

FRUIT FLIES

What They Look Like

The easiest way to tell a fruit fly from another fly is by its habits. If you leave ripe fruit out in the open in summer, the flies you'll find landing on it are most likely fruit flies. They're about the size of the head of a pin, brown-bodied, and have wings. The most common kind has bright red eyes. They're tiny eyes, but you can see them. Female fruit flies with eggs inside have white full-looking bellies. The back ends of males have a blackish tip.

Fruit flies are much more charming than their pesky relatives the house flies, horse flies, blow flies, and mosquitoes. (Yes, mosquitoes are flies.) Fruit flies make no buzzing noise, they don't bite, and they don't hover around people. Best of all, they don't carry germs on their feet, like the flies that land on dead animals or on dog droppings. Fruit flies eat only fruit, which doesn't have bacteria or germs that could make people sick.

Some fruit flies are wingless. They look like miniature Super Mario Bros.™ speeding evenly over the tabletop. With a Mario brother leap, they're up and over your chasing fingertips. They're fast, and amazingly good at avoiding capture. But once you've got them in hand, they're perfectly willing to walk on your skin. Play a game with a friend. See who can keep one from falling the longest!

Class:
Insecta
Order:
Diptera (flies)
Family:
Drosophilidae (fruit flies)
Genus:
Drosophila *species*
Characteristics:
Yellowish or brown flies, $\frac{1}{16}$ to $\frac{1}{8}$ inch (2 to 4 mm) long, with red eyes. Hover around rotting or overripe fruit.
Distribution:
Throughout the United States.
Food:
Rotting fruit.

Fruit Fly

Larva of Fruit Fly

These wingless guys are **mutants**—they're different from other members of their species because of permanent changes in their **genes**. Genes are the elements that control the inheritance of **traits**, or characteristics, from parents to offspring. There are lots of varieties of mutant fruit flies. Some have abnormal eye color or body color, or curly wings, or oddly shaped bristles on their bodies.

Scientists "create" mutant fruit flies by **irradiating** normal fruit flies, exposing them to radiation until one of their genes changes. Then they breed these irradiated flies to study how traits are passed down from parent to offspring, a science called **genetics**. If you take a biology course in high school or college, you may breed your own mutant fruit flies.

Where To Find Them

A picnic outdoors with watermelon or peaches, or a fruit bowl indoors are prime spots for finding fruit flies. If you don't find them right away, leave some ripe fruit outdoors for a few days in warm weather. The softer and smellier it gets, the better they'll like it.

Fruit flies aren't the only flies that eat and lay their eggs on ripe or rotting fruit, but they are by far the most common. The other type of flies found on old fruit are phorid flies, also called humpbacked flies, which are about the same size, but skinnier and gray. Phorid flies don't have the red eyes of fruit flies. Another difference is that fruit flies walk along smoothly unless disturbed, while phorid flies can't seem to get from one place to another without a lot of jerky stops and starts.

If you want the wingless or other mutant variety of fruit flies, you have to order them from a biological supply company (see Appendix).

How to Catch Them

Catching fruit flies is fun. The trap almost always works. I sometimes get a few phorid flies, too, and sometimes a few small sylphid beetles, but always lots of fruit flies. Here's how it works. Get a jar, quart-size or bigger. Large peanut butter jars are great because they're plastic and won't break. Put in the bottom of the jar the rind of half a grapefruit. If you don't

Fruit Flies on Bananas

have a grapefruit, use two or three banana peels. Other fruit will work, but grapefruit works best for me. Then turn the jar on its side, leaving the lid off.

Leave the jar undisturbed for two or three days, until the fruit has gotten mushy and smells stronger. It's important that the jar be in a shaded area or the sun will dry out the fruit. The flies like it best when the fruit has been out two or three days and has gotten mushy and smelly. When you see flies in the jar, get the lid and approach the jar very slowly. Slap the lid on quickly. If you move suddenly around the jar, or bump it or leave it upright instead of on its side, all the flies will escape.

If you try this and don't get any flies, try leaving some fruit outdoors for several days in the area where you plan to leave the jar. This will attract fruit flies to the area. Then remove that fruit and leave your trap. Or try placing your fruit near a garbage can or compost pile where there may be fruit flies already.

How to Keep Them

You can keep the fruit flies in the same jar you trapped them in, but if you move them you'll probably get a better **population** going. A population is a group of interbreeding animals that live together in a particular location. If you want your fruit flies to lay eggs and make more fruit flies, mash an overripe banana into a paste. Put some of the paste into the bottom of a small jar. Sprinkle a tiny pinch of baker's yeast over the paste.

You can move fruit flies from your trap to their new home by knocking them out for a short while. Put your trap in the freezer for a minute or two. When insects get very cold they can't move at all. Don't leave them in the freezer too long. More than three minutes or so may kill them. You can use a cotton swab or small paintbrush to move them around, or just dump them. Cover the top of your new jar or bottle with a piece of cloth, secured with a rubber band.

If the banana paste gets moldy, you'll need to transfer them to a new container with new paste. You can order banana flakes that contain a chemical to keep the paste from getting moldy. See the list of biological supply companies in the Appendix.

What They Act Like

Fruit flies can do tricks without ever leaving their jar. You'll probably notice that most of your fruit flies hang out at the top of the jar, unless they're eating or laying eggs on the paste. Try turning the jar upside down or on its side and see what happens. Do they all run to the new top? Fruit flies have an urge to move up, away from the pull of gravity. This instinct helps them find a good place to launch themselves into flight. Lots of flying insects have the urge to climb.

Fruit flies are popular with biologists because they're easy to raise in containers, and because they make new fruit flies so quickly. Like most animals, fruit flies have to mate to make babies.

Females of all animals are pretty picky about who they mate with, so male animals spend a lot of time strutting around and showing off to impress females. If a female likes a male, she may accept him as her mate. A male bird will show his bright colors and sing to a female to get her attention. A male lizard will push out the brightly colored skin on his throat to say, "Here I am! Please like me." A male frog will puff out his throat and croak for the girls. Male deer will fight and show how strong they are.

Fruit flies are no different. Male fruit flies do a little hop and dance for the girls they hope to win. You can see them doing their little dances in the containers. If you look carefully you'll see a male walking circles or half circles around a female, vibrating his wings. That's his way of saying, "I'm the best male! Let me be your mate!" If she likes his dance, she'll accept him.

Soon after, she will lay eggs. And if you have at least ten flies in your jar, you can be pretty sure at least one will be a female that will successfully mate and lay eggs. The eggs hatch in one day into tiny, white, wormlike larvae. When they're about five days old they're big enough to see, wiggling through the banana paste. A day or two later they crawl up out of the banana paste onto the sides of the jar and turn into little pupae. Fourteen days after the eggs were laid, the skins of the pupae split open and adult flies crawl out. Within a day or two, these new adults mate and lay eggs. So they've gone through the entire life cycle in a little over two weeks.

Sometimes nice things come in small packages, like the tiny little superguy, the fruit fly. He's frisky and full of action—and full of things to do for those of us who like watch nature at work.

APPENDIX

Animals are grouped into categories based on their similarity to one another. The primary, or largest, divisions of the animal kingdom are **phyla**. There are about 26 phyla of animals, depending on whose system of classification you use. Humans are in the phylum Chordata. This phylum includes all animals with backbones and a few other small obscure animals. Another phylum is the mollusks, or Mollusca. This includes octopuses, squids, snails, clams, and other similar animals.

The insects are in the phylum Arthropoda. Some other arthropods are the spiders, the crustaceans, the millipedes, and the centipedes. All the animals in this book are in the phylum Arthropoda. This phylum, and all phyla, are divided into **classes**. The four classes of arthropods described in this book are Insecta (insects), Arachnida (spiders and their kin), Crustacea (crustaceans), and Diplopoda (millipedes).

Each class is divided into **orders**. The insects in this book represent nine orders within the class Insecta, two orders in the class Arachnida, and one order in the class Crustacea. Millipedes occupy an entire class by themselves, the Diplopoda. Orders are further divided into **families**, which are likewise divided into **genera** and, then, **species**. Animals within each division have something in common, such as wing structure. Two animals in the same genus have more features in common than two animals in the same family. Two animals in the same order have more features in common than two animals in the same class, and so on. The only animals that are capable of interbreeding, or mating, successfully are those in the same species.

The system of classification is as follows, with the largest category first and the smallest category last:

Phylum
  Class
    Order
      Family
        Genus
          Species

Phylum Arthropoda

The phylum Arthropoda includes all the animals in this book. It includes insects, spiders, crustaceans, millipedes, and many more. *Arthropoda* means "jointed foot." Arthropods do not have backbones; they have jointed legs and most have an exoskeleton, or hard outer covering made of chitin. This exoskeleton is shed or molted periodically. All have a brain, and a nerve cord that runs along the underside of the body instead of down the back.

Class Insecta

Insects are one group of arthropods. Insects' bodies are divided into three regions: the head, a middle section called the **thorax**, and a rear section called the **abdomen**. Attached to the thorax are three pairs of jointed legs. Most insects, but not all, have two pairs of wings attached to the thorax. Some have one pair of wings, and some have none. Insects have one pair of antennae.

Order Neuroptera

The order Neuroptera includes antlions, lacewings, dobsonflies, snakeflies, and mantidflies. *Neuroptera* means "nerve wings" *(neuro* means "nerve" and *ptera* means "wings"). All have two pairs of clear wings with many visible veins. The network of veins looks like a network of nerves, which is where the name came from. Adults have chewing (as opposed to piercing and sucking) mouthparts, and some are predators. All the larvae are predators. Antennae are long. All neuropterans undergo **complete metamorphosis.** This means that the young, called **larvae**, look very different from the adults. It also means that they go through a **pupal stage** during which the larvae change to the adult form. The insect during this stage is called a **pupa.** Such insects are said to **pupate.**

Order Isoptera

The order Isoptera includes the termites only. *Isoptera* means "equal wings." The name probably comes from the fact that winged termites have only one pair of wings, instead of two different-looking pairs as many other insect orders have.

Termites are social insects, meaning that individuals within the colony have different roles. The colony produces winged individuals at certain times of year, but usually termites are not winged.

Termites are soft-bodied and do not have a narrow waist. They undergo **gradual metamorphosis,** a small change with no pupal stage. The young, which look very much like the adult form, are called **nymphs** instead of larvae.

Order Lepidoptera

This order includes only the butterflies and moths. The name *Lepidoptera* means "scale wings," an appropriate name because the wings, body, and legs are covered with colored scales. The scales come off easily if the butterfly or moth gets stuck in a spider web, helping it escape.

A butterfly or moth has a soft body and a coiled strawlike mouthpart for sucking flower nectar. The long, wormlike larvae, called **caterpillars,** have chewing mouthparts and usually eat leaves. When full size, the caterpillars form an envelope in which to pass the pupal stage. The envelope of moths, called a **cocoon**, is often made of silk, while that of butterflies, called a **chrysalis**, is made of toughened skin. Inside the cocoon or chrysalis, the insects turn into adults. Because they live this pupal stage inside the cocoon, they are said to undergo complete metamorphosis.

Order Diptera

The insect order Diptera includes only the various types of flies, such as house flies, horse flies, crane flies, fruit flies, mosquitoes, midges, gnats, and the like. *Diptera* means "two wings," a name given because they have only two wings. Many other insect orders have two pairs, for a total of four wings. The type of mouthpart varies.

We know the Diptera evolved from insects with two pairs of wings because they still have small knobs in the place where the second pair used to be. These two knoblike organs are called **halteres**, and they are used for balance.

The young are larvae, often called **maggots**. They are usually white and wormlike. Full-sized larvae enter into a pupal stage during which they change into adults, so Diptera undergo complete metamorphosis.

Order Coleoptera

The insect order Coleoptera includes only the beetles. It is the largest order of insects, with over 300,000 species. They have hard bodies and chewing mouthparts. Adults have two pairs of wings. The outer pair are really wing covers, called **elytra**. These form the hard back of the beetle at rest. The name *Coleoptera* means "sheath wings," a reference to these elytra. The inner pair of wings, used for flying, are thin and clear and not visible at rest. In flight, the elytra are flipped up and forward, out of the way.

Beetle larvae are wormlike. Many, such as those of the Japanese Beetle, are called **grubs**. They have a pupal stage and undergo complete metamorphosis. The diet varies.

Order Homoptera

The insect order Homoptera includes the cicadas, leafhoppers, aphids, and scale insects. *Homoptera* means "same wings." The single pair of wings are usually held in a tentlike position over the body. (The lacewings also hold their wings this way, but they're not homopterans.)

Homopterans have a long, stiff, strawlike mouthpart that is used to suck plant juices. This "straw" is usually pulled up against the "chest" when not in use.

The young are called nymphs, and there is no pupal stage. Metamorphosis is gradual.

Order Orthoptera

The insect order Orthoptera includes crickets, grasshoppers, praying mantises, and walkingsticks, among others. *Orthoptera* means "straight wings." All orthopterans have two pairs of wings, but only the front pair are visible when they're not flying. Many "sing" by rubbing one body part against another. Crickets sing or chirp by rubbing one front wing against the other.

All orthopterans have chewing mouthparts (as opposed to piercing or sucking ones), and most eat plants. All have a pair of projections on the back end of the abdomen called **cerci**. The cerci, which are long on crickets, serve as feelers. The cerci on walkingsticks and mantises are shorter but easy to see.

Most orthopterans have long, hairlike antennae, which also serve as feelers. Some use their antennae to communicate with each other by touch.

Class Crustacea

The crustaceans are a large class of mostly aquatic joint-legged animals that have a hard exoskeleton, a pair of appendages (usually legs) on each body segment, and two pairs of antennae. This class includes shrimp, lobsters, crabs, barnacles, and many more. Crustaceans are related to insects because they're both in the phylum Arthropoda, the joint-legged animals with exoskeletons. But insects are not crustaceans, and crustaceans are not insects.

Order Isopoda

The order Isopoda is a large order within the class Crustacea. There are 4,000 species of isopods that live in the ocean and some species that live in fresh water. This order includes the pillbugs and sowbugs, the only truly land-dwelling crustaceans.

All isopods have seven body segments, each bearing a pair of similar legs. The bodies of many isopods are somewhat flattened, as though a finger had pressed on them from above. Isopods' eyes are not on stalks as are those of many crustaceans.

Class Arachnida

This is a class of mostly air-breathing, joint-legged animals. It includes the spiders and scorpions, mites, ticks, and harvestmen. The body of arachnids is divided into two regions, the abdomen and a front region called the **cephalothorax**, which bears four pairs of legs but no antennae. In some the two body regions appear to be fused.

Order Araneae

This order contains only the spiders. It is composed of arachnids whose cephalothorax has a shieldlike covering, on which are set the simple eyes, usually eight in number. The jaws are sharp and pointed and used for injecting prey with poison. They have two leglike organs called **pedipalps** near the jaws, used for holding prey and for feeling. The tip of the abdomen usually has three pairs of **spinnerets**, organs that contain silk glands for producing threads of silk. Each spinneret has a nozzlelike opening.

Order Phalangida or Opiliones

This order contains 3,200 species of daddy-long-legs, or harvestmen. There is no waist between the two body regions, so the body is roundish. The legs of most United States species are very long, spindly, and almost hair-thin. The body is held close to the ground, lower than the highest leg joints.

Class Diplopoda

This class includes only the millipedes. *Diplopoda* means "double foot," a name that refers to the two pairs of legs per body segment. There are more than 7,500 species of millipedes in the world. Some are cylinder-shaped, others are flat. All are long and many-legged. Millipedes are secretive and avoid light. They live under leaves, stones, bark, logs, and in soil.

TO ORDER MANTIS EGG CASES, FRUIT FLIES, MEALWORMS, AND MORE:

Carolina Biological Supply
2700 York Road
Burlington, NC 27215
800/584-0381
North Carolina customers call 800/632-1231

Powell Laboratories
19355 McLoughlin Boulevard
Gladstone, OR 97027
800/547-1733

GLOSSARY

abdomen The rear section of the body of an insect or other arthropod, behind the thorax.

accelerate To gain speed; to go faster.

acceleration The rate of change of speed with time.

adaptation A particular feature of an organism that enables it to survive in its natural environment.

arthropod Any of a phylum of animals without backbones that have jointed legs and usually an exoskeleton, usually made of chitin, that is shed at intervals. Includes insects, spiders, crustaceans, millipedes, centipedes and more.

Batesian mimicry See **mimicry**.

bioluminescence Light produced by living things.

bunching Grouping together in a pile to keep from drying out; a behavior of pillbugs.

camouflaged To be disguised or invisible by looking like the natural surroundings.

caste Any of a particular body type—such as king, queen, worker, or soldier—that has a particular job in a colony of social insects.

caterpillar The long, wormlike larva of a butterfly or moth.

cephalothorax One of two body regions of spiders and their relatives that bears four pairs of legs but no antennae.

cerci (singular *cercus*) A pair of projections on the back end of the abdomen of some insects and other arthropods. Some cerci are used as feelers.

chitin A substance that forms part of the exoskeleton of arthropods. It is shed periodically.

chrysalis A pupa of a butterfly, enclosed in an envelope of hardened skin. The enclosure is also called a chrysalis.

class A major category of biological classification ranking above an order and below a phylum, and composed of related orders.

cocoon An envelope, often made of silk, that a moth larva forms around itself and in which it passes the pupal stage.

colony A population of social insects that live together and interact, and are made up of castes.

complete metamorphosis See **metamorphosis**.

compound eye An eye (as of an insect) made up of many separate visual units.

108

cornicles The pair of sticklike projections off the rear of an aphid's body.

courtship A behavior of mature male and female animals that signals to one another their species' identity and mating readiness. Within a given species, courtship behaviors are usually predictable and consistent.

decompose To undergo chemical breakdown due to the action of bacteria, fungi, and so on.

decomposer Living things, including bacteria, fungi, and such insects as termites, that feed on and break down the remains of dead organisms so that the nutrients in the dead things are recycled and space is made for new living things to grow.

division of labor The assigning of different jobs to different individuals or castes within a population or colony.

ecology The branch of science concerned with the relationship between living things and their environment. Ecologists try to learn which factors in the environment control where animals live and how many of them survive.

ecosystem All of the living and nonliving things in a given location, which interact with each other, depend on one another, and function as a unit.

elytra The outer pair of a beetle's wings that function as wing covers and form the hard back of the beetle at rest.

evolution The theory that the various types of living things are descended from earlier different types of animals and plants. The differences between present-day populations and past populations are due to small changes in one generation after another.

evolve To undergo changes over millions of years that adapt a species more closely to its changing environment.

exoskeleton The hard outer covering of an arthropod's body.

family A category of biological classification ranking above a genus and below an order, and usually composed of several genera.

forage To wander in search of food.

fras The feces, or bodily waste, of a caterpillar.

fungus (plural *fungi)* Any of a major group of organisms, neither plant nor animal, that live on decaying matter. Includes molds, mildew, and mushrooms.

gene An element that controls the inheritance of traits from parents to offspring. A gene is part of a chromosome. Each human cell has, for example, 46 chromosomes, except sperm and egg cells which have 23.

genetics A branch of biology that deals with the inheritance of traits from parent to offspring.

genus (plural **genera**) A category of biological classification ranking above a species and below a family, and composed of related species.

gradual metamorphosis See **metamorphosis**.

grub The wormlike larva of many types of beetles, such as the Japanese Beetle.

halteres A pair of knoblike organs on a fly that are modified second wings and are used for balance.

hibernation The deep sleep many animals go into during winter.

incomplete metamorphosis See **metamorphosis**.

instinct An inherited and automatic behavior that develops in a very predictable way within a particular species.

introduced species A plant or animal that has been brought to one region of the world from another.

irradiate To expose to radiation for the purpose of causing a mutation, a change in the genes.

king The adult male of social insects, who mates with the queen to fertilize her eggs.

larva Any immature insect that is very different in shape from the adult and that undergoes complete metamorphosis.

luciferase An enzyme (a type of protein) that causes luciferin to undergo a chemical change and give off light.

luciferin A pigment that produces light (but no heat) when it undergoes a chemical change called oxidation.

maggots Fly larvae, usually white and wormlike.

membrane A thin layer of skin or tissue on a plant or animal.

metamorphosis A change in body form during development. A gradual and small change, as occurs with mantises, walkingsticks, and crickets, is called **gradual** (or incomplete) **metamorphosis**. An abrupt and great change, as occurs in the chrysalis of a butterfly or cocoon of a lacewing, is called **complete metamorphosis**.

migrate To travel each year from one region or climate to another for feeding or breeding.

mimicry The resemblance of an organism to some other organism or object in the environment, evolved to deceive predators or prey into confusing the organism and that which it mimics. Mimicry in which the original tastes bad and the mimic tastes good is called **Batesian mimicry**

after Henry Bates, the nineteenth-century English naturalist who first described it. Mimicry in which both original and mimic taste bad is called *Mullerian mimicry* after Fritz Muller, the nineteenth-century Brazilian zoologist who first worked it out.

Mullerian mimicry See *mimicry*.

mutant An animal that is different from other members of its species because of permanent changes in its genes.

native species A plant or animal that lives naturally in the area in which it first appeared.

nectar A sugary substance produced by flowers.

noxious Physically harmful to living beings.

nymph The young stage of any insect species that undergoes incomplete or gradual metamorphosis, a slow change without a pupal stage.

offspring The children of an animal or plant.

order A category of biological classification ranking above a family and below a class, and composed of related families.

ovipositor An egg-depositor that some insects, such as crickets, use to lay eggs.

pedipalps The leglike organs near the jaws of spiders and their relatives that are used for holding prey and for feeling.

pheromone The scent produced by an animal that causes another individual of the same species to respond in a particular way.

phylum (plural *phyla*) One of the primary divisions of the animal kingdom.

plankton The weakly swimming or floating tiny animals and plants in a body of water.

population A group of interbreeding animals that live together in a particular location.

predator An animal that kills and eats other animals.

prey An animal taken by another animal, a predator, as food.

pupal stage The stage of development, in insects with complete metamorphosis, where the larva changes to the adult form. The insect during this stage is called a *pupa*. Such insects are said to *pupate*.

pupil The black opening in the center of the eye.

queen The fertile female of social insects, who is bigger than other individuals in the colony and whose only function is to lay eggs The queen is fed and tended by workers.

recoil To be pushed back suddenly by pressure, as when the click beetle's back is pushed against the ground before the beetle leaps.

scale insects Small homopterans that feed on plants. Many are legless, and stay in one spot, and have a scalelike covering.

silk gland A gland that produces a thread of silk. It is enclosed in an organ called a spinneret.

social insects The ants, bees, termites, and wasps, all of which live in colonies with complex social lives.

soldier A member of a colony of social insects who uses its large head and jaws to defend the colony by attacking and biting enemies. Soldiers are not able to reproduce.

specialization Restriction of an organism's activities to a portion of the environment. As used here, restricted to only one or two types of prey.

species (plural **species**) A category of biological classification ranking below a genus, and composed of animals or plants capable of inter-breeding.

spinneret An organ with a nozzlelike opening which contains silk glands for producing threads of silk. The spinnerets of caterpillars are near the mouth. Those of spiders are on the tip of the abdomen.

swarm A large number of animals massed together and usually in motion.

terrarium An enclosure for keeping or raising and observing animals or plants indoors, usually made of clear plastic or glass within a metal frame. It is not filled with water.

thorax The middle of the three main divisions of the body of an insect to which are attached three pairs of jointed legs and, on some insects, one or two pairs of wings.

trait An inherited characteristic.

worker A member of a colony of social insects whose job is to feed and tend the queen and her eggs and larvae, and to make repairs on the nest and so on.

FOR FURTHER READING

The following are similar books you may enjoy.

Borror, Donald, and Richard White. *A Field Guide to Insects—America North of Mexico.* Peterson Field Guide Series. Boston: Houghton Mifflin, 1970.
This is the standard insect field guide in my mind, and the one that I use most often.

Goor, Ron and Nancy. *Insect Metamorphosis.* New York: Macmillan, 1990.
This book has fantastic color photographs of an assortment of insects in various life stages. A beautiful coverage of insect life cycles.

Kneidel, Sally Stenhouse. *Creepy Crawlies and the Scientific Method.* Golden, CO: Fulcrum Publishing, 1983.
This book describes activities and science projects you can do with some common insects and a few other animals.

Lavies, Bianca. *Backyard Hunter, Praying Mantis.* New York: Dutton,1990.
Impressive color photographs of mantises in every stage of life, including hatching from the egg case. There isn't a better book on mantises.

3M. *Compost Critters.* New York: Dutton, 1993.
Most of the book is about the animals that live in and feed on compost and how they break it down. Beautiful color photographs.

Leahy, Christopher. *Peterson First Guide to Insects of North America.* Boston: Houghton Mifflin, 1987.
A much more limited insect field guide than the standard Peterson guide by Borror and White. But it's probably easier for children to use and fits easily into a shirt pocket.

Milne, Lorus and Margery. *The Audubon Society Field Guide to North American Insects and Spiders.* New York: Alfred A. Knopf, 1990.
This is a fun book for browsing, because all the illustrations are color photographs.

Milord, Susan. *The Kids' Nature Book*. Charlotte, VT: Williamson
Publishing, 1989.
This book has a different format. It describes one nature activity for
each day of the calendar year.

Rights, Mollie. *Beastly Neighbors*. Boston: Little, Brown, and Co., 1981.
This book describes not only animals but plants, and has many
chapters devoted to activities such as composting and gardening.

Shepherd, Elizabeth. *No Bones*. New York: Macmillan Publishing Co.,
1988.
This book describes commonly found small arthropods—animals
without backbones. Some are insects.

Sisson, Edith S. *Nature with Children of All Ages*. Englewood Cliffs, NJ:
Phalarope Books, Prentice-Hall, Inc., 1982.
This book covers not only animals, but plants, rocks, sand, seashells,
and more.

Stokes, Donald. *A Guide to Observing Insect Lives*. Boston: Little, Brown,
and Co., 1983.
This book has a lot of detailed information about insect behavior
and life histories for the very curious.

White, Richard. *A Field Guide to the Beetles*. Peterson Field Guide series.
Boston: Houghton Mifflin, 1983.
A thorough enough coverage of beetles, with much more informa-
tion on this group than in an insect field guide.

Zim, Herbert, and Clarence Cottam. *Insects*. Racine, WI: Golden Press of
Racine Publishing Co., 1987.
This is a simpler guide than the standard Peterson guide, and more
usable for children.

INDEX